PENGUIN CLASSICS

FEAR AND TREMBLING

SØREN AABYE KIERKEGAARD was born in Copenhagen in 1813, the youngest of seven children. His mother, his sisters and two of his brothers all died before he reached his twenty-first birthday. Kierkegaard's childhood was an isolated and unhappy one, clouded by the religious fervour of his father. He was educated at the School of Civic Virtue and went on to enter the university, where he read theology but also studied the liberal arts and science. In all, he spent seven years as a student, gaining a reputation both for his academic brilliance and for his extravagant social life. Towards the end of his university career he started to criticize the Christianity upheld by his father and to look for a new set of values. In 1841 he broke off his engagement to Regine Olsen and devoted himself to his writing. During the next ten years he produced a flood of discourses and no fewer than twelve major philosophical essays, many of them written under *noms de plume*. Notable are *Either/Or* (1843), *Repetition* (1843), *Fear and Trembling* (1843), *Philosophical Fragments* (1844), *The Concept of Anxiety* (1844), *Stages on Life's Way* (1845), *Concluding Unscientific Postscript* (1846) and *The Sickness unto Death* (1849). By the end of his life Kierkegaard had become an object of public ridicule and scorn, partly because of a sustained feud that he had provoked in 1846 with the satirical Danish weekly the *Corsair*, partly because of his repeated attacks on the Danish State Church. Few mourned his death in November 1855, but during the early twentieth century his work enjoyed increasing acclaim and he has done much to inspire both modern Protestant theology and existentialism. Today Kierkegaard is attracting increasing attention from philosophers and writers 'inside' and outside the postmodern tradition.

ALASTAIR HANNAY was born to Scottish parents in Plymouth, Devon, in 1932 and educated at the Edinburgh Academy, the University of Edinburgh and University College London. In 1961 he became a resident of Norway, where he is now Emeritus Professor of Philosophy at the University of Oslo. A Fellow of the Royal Society of Edinburgh, he has been a frequent visiting professor at the University of California, at San Diego and at Berkeley. Alastair Hannay has also translated

Kierkegaard's *Either/Or*, *The Sickness unto Death*, *Papers and Journals* and *A Literary Review* for Penguin Classics. His other publications include *Mental Images – A Defence*, *Kierkegaard (Arguments of the Philosophers)*, *Human Consciousness* and *Kierkegaard: A Biography*, as well as articles on diverse themes in philosophical collections and journals. He is the editor of *Inquiry*.

KIERKEGAARD

*

FEAR AND TREMBLING

Dialectical Lyric by
Johannes *de silentio*

*

Translated with an introduction by
Alastair Hannay

PENGUIN BOOKS

PENGUIN BOOKS

Published by the Penguin Group

Penguin Books Ltd, 80 Strand, London WC2R 0RL, England

Penguin Group (USA) Inc., 375 Hudson Street, New York, New York 10014, USA

Penguin Group (Canada), 90 Eglinton Avenue East, Suite 700, Toronto, Ontario, Canada M4P 2Y3
(a division of Pearson Penguin Canada Inc.)

Penguin Ireland, 25 St Stephen's Green, Dublin 2, Ireland (a division of Penguin Books Ltd)

Penguin Group (Australia), 707 Collins Street, Melbourne, Victoria 3008, Australia
(a division of Pearson Australia Group Pty Ltd)

Penguin Books India Pvt Ltd, 11 Community Centre, Panchsheel Park, New Delhi – 110 017, India

Penguin Group (NZ), 67 Apollo Drive, Rosedale, Auckland 0632, New Zealand
(a division of Pearson New Zealand Ltd)

Penguin Books (South Africa) (Pty) Ltd, Block D, Rosebank Office Park,
181 Jan Smuts Avenue, Parktown North, Gauteng 2193, South Africa

Penguin Books Ltd, Registered Offices: 80 Strand, London WC2R 0RL, England

www.penguin.com

This translation first published 1985
Reprinted with a new Chronology 2003

055

Printed and bound in Great Britain by Clays Ltd, Elcograf S.p.A.

Set in Monophoto Photina

ISBN-13: 978-0-140-44449-0

www.greenpenguin.co.uk

MIX
Paper from
responsible sources
FSC   FSC™ C018179

Penguin Books is committed to a sustainable
future for our business, our readers and our planet.
This book is made from Forest Stewardship
Council™ certified paper.

CONTENTS

INTRODUCTION

God said to Abraham, go kill me a son.
Abe said, Man, you must be puttin' me on.
BOB DYLAN, *Highway 61*

The Old Testament story of Abraham's journey to the mountain
to sacrifice Isaac has been read in widely different ways. It was
used by the early Christian Church to celebrate faith and
obedience. The focus then was on Abraham and his unreserved
submission to God's will. In Jewish culture the story was later
used to invoke God's mercy: instead of the hand raised in
sacrifice, it was the staying of the hand that assumed importance, when the angel said, 'Lay not thine hand upon the lad,
neither do thou any thing unto him'.* Faith, obedience, and
mercy are social virtues. For a modern consciousness the story
is likely to be read as an anti-social parable of destruction and
raw power. The opening verse of Bob Dylan's song concludes,
'God said, you can do what you want, Abe, but next time you
see me comin', you'd better run. Well, Abe said, where you want
this killin' done? God said, do it on Highway 61'. Faith, obedience, and mercy have here given way to disbelief, arbitrariness,
and intimidation.

Abraham's journey is the centrepiece of Kierkegaard's *Fear and
Trembling*. But Kierkegaard's focus, as originally, is on Abraham;
Isaac is little more than a foil to Abraham's 'greatness'. Yet this
greatness is not, as in the traditional reading, Abraham's
willingness to be an instrument of God's omnipotence. Kierkegaard's Abraham is great because of what he suffers in a trial
of faith. And far from epitomizing social virtues, this Abraham's
suffering and greatness seem to isolate him in a very radical
way from his society and its social ways. In impressing us with
Abraham's greatness Kierkegaard has a very special purpose.
In fact one can safely say that *Fear and Trembling* is not primarily

* Genesis 22.12.

concerned with the story of Abraham and Isaac at all; it uses
the story in order to draw the reader's attention to certain very
fundamental questions. The work has a polemical purpose and
to carry it out Kierkegaard requires us to focus on the nature
of the suffering involved in the story. In this introduction I shall
explain these features more fully, indicating in some detail the
background to Kierkegaard's writings.

Fear and Trembling first appeared in Copenhagen bookshops
on 16 October 1843, along with a companion work, *Repetition*,
and a collection of 'Edifying Discourses'. The first two works
were written under false names, 'Johannes *de silentio*' and
'Constantin Constantius', a practice followed by Kierkegaard in
all the works he later called his 'aesthetic production', from
Either/Or (1843) to *Practice in Christianity* (1850). According
to its subtitle, *Fear and Trembling* is a 'dialectical lyric'. That
doesn't mean that *Fear and Trembling* is a mainly literary work
to be judged by standards of style and presentation, or its topic
largely a medium for the artistic development of a literary talent.
Since it does call itself a lyric, however, we would certainly
expect its author to want his handiwork to be judged at least
partly by such standards. Indeed all of Kierkegaard's 'aesthetic'
works are products of someone obviously delighting in his native
literary talent. But to read them as purely literary exercises
would be misconceived as well as frustrating. Misconceived
because, far from being a mere vehicle for literary expression,
their themes are very obviously the author's main concern
throughout, and where the style may be called literary, that
fact is to be seen rather in the light of the author's chosen way
of bringing those themes to light. Frustrating because unless
the reader gets a firm hold of the theme and its not always
immediately transparent ramifications, much of the work will
defy the kind of immediate recognition of meaning on which
literary presentation depends.

What Kierkegaard means by 'aesthetic' is not altogether
removed from the idea of appreciation of beauty. It is, one could
say, his characterization of a way of life in which anything at
all, and not just what we reserve for labels like 'art', 'beauty',
and 'good taste', is treated aesthetically. To treat something

aesthetically is to grasp it in terms of the immediate impact it makes, of how it strikes you in the here and now, of its tendency to attract or repel you. In a more general way it is, in Kierkegaard's terms, also to treat life itself as a repository of objects of longing or loathing, as well as degrees of lesser affect in between, in short as a pool of goods (of whatever kind) to be secured and the lack of them avoided. The aesthetic life is a life dedicated to what Kierkegaard calls 'immediacy'. The word is taken from Hegel, for whom it means unreflective knowledge, in which – and this is vital in what follows – he includes faith. In his major 'dialectical' work, *Concluding Unscientific Postscript*, Kierkegaard describes a person dedicated to the life of immediacy as being 'absolutely committed to relative ends'.* The idea of absolute commitment to something relative is intended to smack of contradiction, as it surely does, and finding some suitable expression for the conflict here will give us our first taste of the theme of *Fear and Trembling*. The simplest but in most ways least suitable expression for it is 'faith'. The word is not only very imprecise; it would be wrong to think of the work as being concerned with faith as such, in some general or particular sense, and not rather with making some point *about* faith. The suitable expression we need is one that says what kind of faith Kierkegaard has in mind and what, in the words of his pseudonym, he wants to say about it.

But we have one more packet to open. Can we assume that it is possible to say anything at all about faith? Here we need to call attention to the Hegelian background for Kierkegaard's writings. Hegel certainly thought one could talk about faith. But that was because Hegel considered his own philosophy to provide a general vantage-point from which it was in principle possible to discern the true character of all topics 'proper' to forms of consciousness other than the philosophical. Hegel discusses two such alternative forms of consciousness: the experience of art and beauty ('aesthetics' in the usual, narrower sense) and religious experience. For Hegel these are not alternatives in the sense that they form equally valid routes to

Concluding Unscientific Postscript, trans. D. F. Swenson and W. Lowrie, Princeton University Press, Princeton, N.J., 1941, p. 412.

knowledge or understanding. The best that either can afford in this respect is a truncated, and in essential ways distorted, vision of the truth. A complete and undistorted vision, or at any rate an adequate grasp of the possibility of such a vision, Hegel calls the Absolute Mind. The Absolute Mind is a rational mind. Art is one way in which the Absolute Mind manifests itself in human consciousness, but only in an opaque fashion. In the experience of beauty, and more especially in art than in nature, the rational appears in bodily form to our senses. Religion is a better but still opaque medium for Absolute Mind. Here the rational appeals both to the senses and to the intellect in so far as it is given a narrative structure, which in Christianity comes as far to approximating the Absolute Mind's vision as is possible in this form of consciousness. But the content is still only symbolic or pictorial. Philosophy is the highest manifestation of the Absolute Mind, and here all that art manifests and all that religion manifests of the Absolute Mind acquires its adequate, rational expression. Naturally then, the Hegelian regards religious faith as a provisional state of mind. In order to grasp reality in the manner appropriate to the rational reality it is, one must *go further*, one must proceed to the point of view of philosophy, and there one will be able to convert one's religious faith into what that phenomenon 'really' is, and whatever that is it is not what it was for one who had it. Then one will not only have gone further than faith, but also put faith in its proper perspective in the (fundamentally rational) scheme of things. One will have put it, moreover, in the form of concepts, transcribed it into the form of shareable thoughts in the words of a common language.

We notice that Kierkegaard has given his author the name 'Johannes *de silentio*', which is allegedly borrowed from one of the Grimms' fairy-tales, 'The Faithful Servant'.* Kierkegaard's John of Silence is not, however, at all a silent person. If he was he wouldn't be an author. Nor was the faithful servant in the

---

*The claim for this origin is made by E. Hirsch in *Teologisk Tidsskrift for den danske Folkekirke* (1931), pp. 214 ff. I owe the information to Niels Thulstrup's commentary to his Danish edition of *Fear and Trembling*, Gyldendals Uglebøger, Copenhagen, 1968, p. 164.

fairy-tale. He told his master, the young king, of three dangers threatening him, though realizing that in doing so he would be turned to stone. (To anticipate a further connection with *Fear and Trembling*, when the royal couple later got two sons they gave the lives of these in sacrifice in order to bring Johannes back to life, whereupon Johannes brought the children back to life.) Johannes, the author, is no slouch with words; and yet he finds it difficult to say anything about faith except that it is something which, if you have it, you will not be able to explain to anyone else. Instead of seeing faith from some elevated point of view like that of Hegel's 'System' (Hegel's own word for the complete account of the ascent to the Absolute Mind's transparency), Kierkegaard's author conveys to us the hard fact that faith, if it is anything, simply has no place in a system of thought, that 'faith begins precisely where thinking leaves off'. Faith, for Johannes *de silentio*, is an expression rather of the limit of what can be thought. A person who has it cannot say what it is he has; or at least he cannot say what faith is from any 'systematic' or scientific point of view. (We should note that Hegel also thought of his system as a *science*, the science of spirit.) But having read *Fear and Trembling* we might even suppose that Kierkegaard has wanted his pseudonym to tell us that if someone genuinely has faith, as Abraham the father of Isaac is said to have proved by his willingness to sacrifice Isaac, then that person has in that respect exiled himself from the realm of human discourse. His faith is an affront to humanity as we generally understand this, that is as a more or less well-defined set of dispositions that we expect or recognize in each other and value.

There may be doubts (there is certainly controversy) as to the precise extent of the unintelligibility that Kierkegaard would have his author attribute to the having of faith. But the general drift of *Fear and Trembling*'s treatment of faith is clear enough: if we are to talk of faith at all it is of something we cannot explain in any language that suffices for people to describe and justify their actions and attitudes to one another. *Fear and Trembling* has a Preface which says that faith in Kierkegaard's time is thought to be where one begins in life, not where one aims to end. A parallel is drawn with doubt. The Greek sceptics strove all their lives to retain their suspension of judgement, and thus as they saw it their peace of mind, against every pressure that threatened to extort a decision from them in some matter of controversy. Doubt was what they sought to preserve, not a state of immaturity they felt bound to overcome. So too with the prevalent Hegelian notion of faith. It is not grasped as something hard to come by. To be able to believe, as Johannes says in his Preface that his contemporaries do, that faith is the beginning and not the end one must have a cheapened conception of faith. One must think of faith as a state of a certain kind which it is right and proper for mature human beings to overcome. Faith is then not the highest one can aspire to, as it was for former generations; nor therefore are the goals contemporaries set themselves the same as those set by generations for whom faith was a 'task for a whole life-time'. Take Abraham, the 'father of faith'. His faith is said to have been put to the test by God. A grim test by any standards. Abraham has to be prepared, to the point of actually performing the deed, to kill his only and much-loved son Isaac. Abraham withstood the test, but was allowed at the last moment to sacrifice a ram instead, and has ever after been celebrated as the worthy father of the nations and families descended from his son. But the celebration is performed merely in words. We not only do not understand what Abraham went through, we are led by Hegelian philosophy to suppose that we have the measure of Abraham's greatness and that the faith Abraham bore witness to is to be treated as though it were 'a children's disease which one must hope to get over as soon as possible'. In an Epilogue Johannes *de silentio* asks whether the only way to raise the value of what we consider to be human ideals is to be less complacent, more critical, about having already attained them – if for no other reason than 'to have something to fill the time with', i.e. by taking up the slack. He offers an alternative, to see what life's problems and tasks *really* are, to keep them fresh in mind, and to bear in mind that they are not to be solved and performed by acquiring new forms of consciousness in which the problems and tasks virtually disappear as they do for Hegelians, so that succeeding generations inherit the solutions without having to face the problems.

The most embracing general message of *Fear and Trembling* seems to be, then, that the notion of faith is in current discussion of it so far cheapened that what is talked about is not properly called faith at all; and that if we are to praise venerable figures like Abraham, or Abraham in particular since he is revered as the father of faith, we should be made to appreciate what it was like to be Abraham undergoing the trial of faith. If Abraham is to be said to be great, then we should be given a clear picture of what it was that he achieved. This Johannes *de silentio* sets out to do in the first of *Fear and Trembling*'s two fairly neat divisions. This first part is lyrical rather than dialectical. We are 'tuned' to the right frame of mind in a short section which presents four different versions of the Abraham and Isaac story, all of which would make Abraham intelligible to us but none of which would make him the father of faith. Our author presents the four versions as imagined by someone who was first gripped by the story as a child but later, without losing his sense of the grandeur of Abraham, has grown increasingly perplexed about what Abraham actually did, and tries to put himself in the position of an observer of the events – not, we are told, to add the detail of immediate experience to his earlier fascination, but to try to grasp in *thought* what happened, an attempt which Johannes *de silentio* as it were takes over and whose nature earns for his 'lyric' the qualification 'dialectical'. There follows a 'speech in praise of Abraham'. The notion of speech is central to Johannes *de silentio*'s 'lyrical' effort at conveying to us what Abraham actually went through. (Which is why I have not translated the Danish 'Lovtale' as is customary with 'eulogy' or 'panegyric'.) *Fear and Trembling* has as its central (as opposed to enveloping) concern the question of whether what faith is, if it is anything, can be *spoken* about. The conclusion appears to be that it cannot. But we can certainly speak about Abraham. We can speak about him in many ways. Unthinkingly as the child hearing the story for the first time, and who has not yet learned the distinctions we employ when adult; or – as our author goes on in a more ironic vein to point

out in the following section – in the way of the cleric who knows
the distinctions but fails to apply them as he goes through the
verbal motions of praising Abraham in his Sunday sermon; or,
as we are told in the 'speech', in the way of the poet who sees
in his hero a better nature that he might himself have aspired
to but as a poet prefers merely to commemorate by giving
expression to. Johannes *de silentio* takes us further than all of
these. He tries to convey what it must have meant to Abraham
to be told by God that he was to sacrifice Isaac, to want to bear
witness to his faith but to be able to do so only by putting his
own son to death. Abraham could have been great in a number
of ways. He might have sacrificed himself instead. Or sacrificed
Isaac but in resignation rather than faith (see below). But his
special greatness was that, in doing what he did, he did not
doubt that he would get Isaac back. Abraham believed he would,
if not keep Isaac, at least have him restored, whatever he did,
even to the point of killing him. His greatness was to be able
to keep that faith in that circumstance and in the context of
all that Isaac meant to him, and thus in full view of the extent
of his loss if his belief should be unfounded. The result of
Johannes *de silentio*'s speech in praise of Abraham is to establish
his greatness on three counts: in respect of what he loved (God),
of what he confidently expected (the impossible), and of what
he strove with (not the world, or himself, but again God). The
sum of what Johannes *de silentio* can say here is that Abraham
was willing, and in the most extreme test imaginable proved
himself able, to accept that human life, Isaac's, Abraham's,
everyone's, acquires its meaning and value from the source of
creation itself, not from 'the raging elements and forces of
creation' that confront a person and bear him along in the world,
both outside and in the 'dark passions' inside his own soul.

But although our author can admire Abraham for this, there
is still the question of whether he can understand him. This
question is raised in the second, more properly 'dialectical' part
of *Fear and Trembling*. This part opens with a 'Preamble from
the Heart' (*Foreløbig Expectoration*, lit. 'preliminary unbosoming', usually rendered, misleadingly for English ears, as 'preliminary expectoration') that sets the stage by giving graphic

accounts of the distinctions we need to understand what 'faith' means in this context. By 'dialectic' Kierkegaard means something not far removed from what modern philosophers would call 'conceptual analysis', or the clarification of distinctions, though here distinctions hard to face rather than hard to make. The most manifest aim of the section, called 'Problemata', to which the unbosoming is a 'preliminary' is to show that if Abraham is indeed to be praised for the specific greatness attributed to him in the 'speech', then certain central principles of Hegelian philosophy are untenable. Conversely, if they are tenable, then Hegelians should not be paying lip service to Abraham's greatness. The principles are taken up in the three *problemata* which form the dialectical part proper of *Fear and Trembling*.

According to Hegel's concept of what he calls 'the ethical life' (*Sittlichkeit*) behaviour is moral when it contributes to the maintenance of the ethical unit formed by any society. Actions undertaken by the individual on his own behalf lack a moral aspect unless they can be linked, in intention and/or fact, to the well-being of society as a whole; and an individual who feels unbound by ties of association and duty (at least to his associates), or does not see the necessity in respect of his *own* well-being of personal participation in the social whole, lacks insight into the true, 'rational' relationship between an individual and society, or, in the terminology both Hegel and Kierkegaard use, between 'particular' and 'universal'. (I have translated 'den Enkelte' as 'the single individual', though occasionally also as 'particular', and not just as 'the individual', since Kierkegaard sometimes refers to the individual, or *Individet*, in contexts where the distinction between an individual-as-particular's being and not being constituted in the universal is not the issue. And I have translated 'det Almene' as 'the universal' even though this is misleading if it suggests absolute generality in a logical universe; in Hegel and in Kierkegaard 'universal' is related to the notion of 'whole' as opposed to 'part' or at most to what applies generally within a concrete domain, e.g. a society or nation.) In *Fear and Trembling* the requirement of ethics is stated – though perhaps only postulated (see below)

– as being that the individual should be 'doing something for the universal'. According to this view, to do what would normally count as contrary to your duties can only be justified if there is some wider benefit to the universal at stake. Thus you may be called upon in the service of the State to act contrary to your obligations as a father or mother. If what you are called upon to do is, say, sign a death-warrant for the execution of your son, you will be exonerated for that aspect of your action which would otherwise be labelled a moral outrage against your child (and the society of which the child is of course also a member). Indeed not only will you be exonerated but acclaimed as a kind of moral hero. But if you were to carry out that same aspect of the action outside such a context, and if there were nothing in the action that counted as doing something for the universal, then ethically speaking you would be damned.

But that is just Abraham's situation. He is prepared to kill his own son even though in doing so he does nothing for the universal. Indeed, as our author points out, there is an added irony in the case of Abraham, since it had been God's promise to him that through Isaac he was to be the progenitor of the nations that are the very repository of any (future) 'universal'. In so far as the universal enters into Abraham's act, it does so only as it lies 'concealed in [Isaac's] loins'. If Abraham's act is not to be simple, or even compound, murder, then there must be some higher court of appeal than that of the ethical life; there must be some authority that can be called absolute in relation to the ethical life, and in relation to which the ethical life is itself merely relative. The situation where that condition is satisfied Johannes *de silentio* calls the 'teleological suspension of the ethical', since in that case the ethical life no longer has its goal within itself, but is subservient as a whole to some other end, or *telos*.

Kierkegaard's use of the Abraham and Isaac story in *Fear and Trembling* has caused much controversy. It has led some to reject Kierkegaard's thought out of hand, as committing him to the view that barbaric acts can be sanctioned by appeal to 'faith'. Others, more inclined to be sympathetic to Kierkegaard from the start, have sought for saving interpretations, for instance in the fact that *Fear and Trembling* is after all the work of a pseudonym and the views expressed (as Kierkegaard expressly says) are not to be identified as Kierkegaard's own, or Kierkegaard was half-poet and so inclined to select his examples for their immediate impact rather than analogical accuracy, or else his concerns are polemical and so the Abraham and Isaac example can be catalogued as strategic exaggeration, and so on. I would not disparage such attempts to save Kierkegaard, or even the decision to reject his thought out of hand; and I certainly would not do so without sufficient space to spread out the various views and assess them. However, it seems to me that such reactions are often based on a failure to look closely enough at the actual text and to follow the argument. The first place to look is at this notion of *faith*. What is it that Abraham is supposed to exemplify?

In his 'Preamble from the Heart' Johannes *de silentio* presents us with a graphically drawn distinction between resignation and faith, represented in the figures of their respective 'knights'. There is no faith, in Kierkegaard's sense, without prior resignation. More than that, there is no faith unless the believer takes with him something essential to the knight of resignation. And there is no resignation unless there is something in the world that a person wants in the strong sense in which one says he or she has set his or her heart on it. Resignation is, as it were, renouncing one's most cherished hopes when whatever is hoped for proves unattainable. Resignation is not giving up thinking about one's heart's desire; on the contrary, being resigned requires retaining the original interest but accepting that nothing on earth will permit it to be satisfied. If you were to accept that it could indeed be satisfied, it could only be 'on the strength of the absurd'. The word 'absurd' here means not 'logically impossible' but 'humanly impossible', or 'in any intelligible way impossible'. When a friend dies one may want more than anything that the friend be restored to life, and of course that is not possible; one could only think it was possible on the strength of the absurd. And if one did think it possible on the strength of the absurd, one would no doubt be convicted of absurdity oneself if one let one's hopes, even expectations,

be known. There is no logical absurdity in the hope or expectation; one doesn't wish that one's friend were both dead and
alive, only alive; but it is nevertheless an absurd hope or
expectation and anyone entertaining such could only do so in
the full consciousness that the absurd must actually take place
for fulfilment to occur. If, for instance, one entertained the hope
or expectation *without* fully facing up to the fact, or conviction,
that its fulfilment is a human impossibility, one would be too
confused to be a knight of resignation. If the case of resurrection
sounds too far-fetched, take our author's own example. A young
man falls in love with a princess but then realizes he has no
prospects there and resigns himself to the impossibility. The idea
of there being any prospects is therefore now absurd. Clearly
it is not a contradiction. Who knows? Perhaps one day he will
find himself in the situation where the princess is no longer
out of bounds. But so long as he is resigned he does not contemplate that possibility. *Faith* is then the young man's ability,
not even just to contemplate the possibility, but to accept that
what is (absurdly) possible is in fact in store for him. As Johannes
de silentio points out, what people often mean by 'faith' is something much less, something one needs '*in order* to renounce
everything', not something that itself presupposes that one *has*
renounced everything.

   Another thing. Faith is almost exclusively linked to the idea
of belief in God's existence. But that is not at all what is meant
here. Johannes *de silentio* envisages the situation had Abraham
only resigned. Resignation for Abraham would not be his denying himself the belief that God exists. According to Johannes,
resignation on Abraham's part would be giving up Isaac *to* God.
The resigned Abraham would *not* expect to get Isaac back. But
that would not be because there was no God to manipulate the
suprahuman possibilities needed to restore Isaac; rather it would
be because God was not the kind of deity one could count on
to be disposed to give back to Abraham his opportunity to
exercise paternal love. The resigned Abraham believes God
wants him to sacrifice Isaac and that the sacrifice will be the
end of Isaac as far as he is concerned. If Abraham did not already
believe in God's existence there would clearly be difficulties. If

the test was a proof of Abraham's belief in the existence of God, who could Abraham suppose set the test? The story says he accepted that God had set it. But then he already believed in God's existence – and that would be just as true even if he failed the test. What the test requires of Abraham is not that he believe that God exists, but that he believe that God both wants and will be able to give him back his opportunity to exercise paternal love. Faith in God's existence is something Abraham already has; the faith he is to prove is his believing that he will not in the end be deprived of Isaac even if he carries out God's command to kill him. 'In the end' does not include 'in the hereafter'. It is, as Johannes *de silentio* says, for *this* life that he believes in the possibility of getting Isaac back on the strength of the absurd. Abraham's trial is to show that he believes that he and Isaac will be living together again even after he has sacrificed Isaac.

We can get nearer to the core of the story in Kierkegaard's version by varying its scenario. Suppose Kierkegaard had indeed intended that the test should be of Abraham's faith in God's existence. That would have meant that Abraham had the option of not believing in the existence of God; and given the nature of the test Abraham would surely find it hard to associate it with belief in any kind of deity that he would *want* to believe existed, so for theoretical reasons as well as to protect Isaac he would no doubt choose not to believe. Suppose, secondly, that Abraham sacrifices Isaac and does not get him back 'in the end'. That might mean that the test was not at all as Abraham supposed. The test could have been to withstand the *temptation* to suspend the ethical teleologically, for God could be a Hegelian who wanted to have proof of Abraham's faith in the rightness of 'accomplishing the universal'. Or suppose, thirdly, that we exclude the possibility of a Hegelian God but still Abraham does not get Isaac back. Could a God such as Abraham believed in demand such an action, intending Abraham to believe he will get Isaac back, and yet not give Isaac back? Or would that (shades of Descartes!*) be some kind of proof that God did not exist?

* In the fourth of his *Meditations on First Philosophy* Descartes argues that if God is perfect he cannot deceive.

Regarding the first supposition, as I have said, it is perfectly clear that Abraham is not to be understood as someone who could decide not to believe that God existed; his choice concerns rather what one is to hope for or expect given that God does exist. Second, it is equally clear that Kierkegaard's God is not Hegel's, but a source of values the realization of which does indeed call for the teleological suspension of the ethical. As for the third and more problematic supposition, it strikes me as desirable, in tackling the question of Kierkegaard's intentions here, to focus on what is actually recounted. Abraham believes he will get Isaac back and he does. The possibility that he might not is one that Abraham chooses to ignore, correctly as it turns out. The point of the story is best sought in these two features.

The 'Preamble from the Heart' gives us a portrait of a knight of faith very different from that of Abraham. There the knight is outwardly indistinguishable from the proverbial man in the street; he seems in fact to be *petit bourgeois* from top to toe, a shopman in the street. He is visibly at home in the world, and attends with all possible enthusiasm to any of life's details. No sign of the faraway look, the resigned detachment, of someone who has given up his hopes for this world; but neither anything to compare with the silent resolution of Abraham. And yet, we are told, this person is at every moment making the 'movement of faith' against the settled conviction that 'humanly speaking' it is absurd that the things he enthuses over should have the value he obviously ascribes to them. The intended analogy with Abraham could be this. Isaac is, in not just the metaphorical sense, the whole world for Abraham (as the promise of future generations he is the whole world also in a wider sense), and the latter's willingness to part with Isaac represents the necessary feature of resignation which is the renunciation of the *human* possibility of possessing 'the whole world'. This feature must be an element in Abraham's faith. But only this feature, not the whole of resignation. Johannes *de silentio*'s knight of resignation, the young man in love with the princess, once he realizes the futility of his love, cancels it as a worldly project and turns his idea of the princess into a kind of attribute of God, directing his love at God instead. Our author says that his love takes on 'the expression of eternal love'. If Abraham were to resign himself to *losing* Isaac he would abandon Isaac to God and direct his love at God, away from the world which now conspicuously lacks all that as a father he loves. But although as a knight of faith he must emulate the knight of resignation in accepting the human impossibility of a continued earthly love of Isaac, precisely as a knight of *faith* he restores his love to its former target, the worldly state, still a human impossibility, but now, on the strength of the absurd, regained in faith as a divine possibility, which he even anticipates as a certainty. Obviously *we* can raise the question, what if his certainty is misplaced?, and speculate about the implications in that event. *Would* it be proof that God did not exist? Or that Abraham was wrong to assume that the best for Isaac and him was that they should stay together, or to assume that it was not better for Isaac to be with God? Would it show that resignation was the appropriate stopping place and faith too far? But these questions I believe distract attention from the features of the story that are meant to be salient. According to these we should see Abraham primarily as in a most definitive way accepting that the good things in life, represented for him in Isaac, derive their value not from the mere fact that they exist and can be valued, enjoyed, delighted in, but from the source of existence itself. Abraham is, as it were, handing Isaac back so as to receive him again on the proper basis.

It can certainly seem that important elements in the Abraham story drop out if we take the analogy between Abraham and the shopman to extend no further than this. In the first place, there is nothing in Johannes *de silentio*'s portrayal of the knight of faith as shopman to suggest *sacrifice*, and Abraham's willingness to sacrifice Isaac is supposed to be the test of his faith. Second, there is nothing in the portrayal of the shopman knight to suggest the breach of *ethical* responsibility that Abraham's sacrifice involves.

Let us briefly consider these two disanalogies. First the element of sacrifice. To make a sacrifice is to give away something or someone of value in an interest that stands higher on the value-scale than the (admittedly already high) interest served by refraining from giving it or the person away. The problem with understanding Abraham is to grasp what that higher interest can be. Sacrifice in a higher cause is a familiar enough occurrence, in history and in myth; usually it is in the interests of the nation or the State, and the sacrifice is made to the (tear-filled) applause of those who identify their own interests with that of the nation or the State. But in sacrificing Isaac Abraham is serving no higher interest of that openly shared kind. No one will applaud him. Now in ordinary life we abandon things and persons for quite selfish reasons. But we would often like to parade these 'losses' as sacrifices on behalf of projects of a not purely selfish nature. A young man might abandon his plans to marry and excuse himself by telling his jilted fiancée that marriage would interfere with his own longer-term interests in being a 'fulfilled' human being, or, still more pompously, with society's interests in the fruits of his further education. He might even try to convince her it was in *her* better interests. For any outsider, including the fiancée, it would be very hard to tell how honest these claims to unselfishness were, or whether the real reason was that the young man was tired of the girl, thinks marriage will bind him, or wants more 'experiences' before 'settling down'.

The Abraham story is not like an everyday one. As Johannes *de silentio* tells it there can be no deception or self-deception of that kind. Abraham could not be wrong in believing that he has no selfish interest to serve in abandoning Isaac. He has only one selfish interest, and that is invested in Isaac. There is nothing Abraham could envisage for his own benefit that was not identical with his hopes for Isaac. There is therefore no basis in Abraham for the general doubt one may entertain about a sacrificer's honesty, that people often do have motives to conceal purely selfish reasons for disregarding the wishes and interests of those whose interests they would be expected to protect. That being so, when we are told that Abraham abandons Isaac in order to prove his faith, we cannot suspect, as in ordinary life we often can, that this is just a cover that serves to conceal some more mundane interest. In intending to kill Isaac Abraham has no other interest than to testify to his faith – which we recall is belief that he is going to keep Isaac in spite of the human impossibility of his doing so if he puts Isaac to death. Note that by being himself the cause of Isaac's death Abraham also eliminates the kind of doubt one can have about a person's faith when it is adopted in order to alleviate the pain, say, of bereavement caused naturally. Here Abraham, by bereaving *himself* of Isaac, is the occasion of the torment that calls for alleviation. His faith cannot be a means of alleviating pain when it is the cause of the pain it is supposed to alleviate. The main point, however, is precisely that the story of Abraham as *Fear and Trembling* presents it is artificially removed from the kinds of context in which sacrifices are normally called for, and from the situations that normally call for them. This allows Abraham to act in a way that unambiguously conveys his belief *about* the things he values, without his personal interest in these infecting the belief in a way that can normally make professions of faith suspect. Of course you might say that the intention to prove his faith is itself a personal interest of Abraham's. That would be the case if, for instance, Abraham acted as he did in order to show God that he was able to obey *any* command of God's, because, as one might say, he fancied himself as a totally obedient servant of God. But in fact there is nothing of this kind to be elicited from the story as we are told it. All we are told is that Abraham wanted to show his faith, and, as we have seen, that faith consists in the belief that he will keep Isaac, or that Isaac will be restored. Normally a sacrificer does not entertain the prospect of receiving again what he parts with. But that is because in the normal case a sacrifice is an act of resignation, not of (Abraham's kind of) faith.

The story of Abraham and Isaac need not be taken, therefore, as a literal description of what a person must be prepared to do if he is to be said to have faith. It can be read as an allegory in which Abraham's actions symbolize some general feature of a religious consciousness rather than illustrate the sort of deeds expected of someone who has that consciousness. What that general feature is might be specified in a variety of ways. In the above I have suggested that it has to do with the assumption

a religious believer must make about the things and persons
he values in the world, and that this assumption can be brought
to light in the case where something or someone a person totally
sets his heart on proves to be humanly speaking unattainable.
This might suggest that faith, the belief that it is nevertheless
to be attained 'on the strength of the absurd', is only for losers,
the young men whose princesses are unavailable, the young
maidens who are doomed never to find husbands (another of
our author's examples). That would be a very narrow concept
of faith (though there is a tendency in Kierkegaard to talk as
if faith was only possible for sufferers). But Johannes *de silentio*'s
'lyrical' account of resignation, too, might be allegorical. It could
be read as symbolizing the way a person must look upon everything that he values, whether or not it is unattainable. It could
symbolize the attitude that says that nothing in the world has
value simply because one values it. This would be resignation
about values generally, as in Max Weber's 'disenchantment'
(*Entzauberung*). Faith would be, correspondingly, the attitudinal
appendix to this, that things have their value nonetheless, but
they have them on their own account and from God. It would
be plausible to attribute this compound attitude to the shopman
knight of faith, but also of course to attribute it to Abraham
and his belief that what he is giving to God will be returned,
as it was but with its status clarified.

There remains the second disanalogy between the shopman
knight and Abraham, namely that there is nothing in Johannes
de silentio's portrayal of the former to suggest a breach with
the ethical. This brings us to the infamous 'teleological suspension of the ethical', the subject, as remarked before, of much
academic controversy. The problem has been to reconcile the
idea that Abraham's sacrifice can be a 'good' action, because in
fulfilment of God's command, with its being an action in total
defiance of any conceivable ethical standard. It is not a sacrifice
that can be defended on the grounds that it recognizably or
even imaginably contributes to the good of some person or
persons whose good might be conceived to stand higher on some
scale of values. Indeed there is no person or persons whom it
benefits at all.

Once more it pays to take heed of what Kierkegaard has his author say. The words are, as always with Kierkegaard, chosen with expert care and used with great consistency. We should first recall what has already been said. The faith that Kierkegaard is concerned with here is not plain belief in the existence of God; it is belief that the projects on which one sets one's heart are possible even when they prove humanly impossible to carry through. It is the belief that they can be carried through, but on a new basis, as once Isaac is restored the project of loving him as befits a father continues but now reconstituted 'on the strength of the absurd'. In the third of the *problemata*, on the question of whether Abraham should have told the affected parties (including of course the sacrificial victim) of his intention to sacrifice Isaac, we are told another story – or rather several versions of another story, that of Agnete and the merman, which unlike the Abraham one is clearly intended to mirror a situation in real life. In drawing his conclusions from this story our author tells us that the greatest person he can conceive of is one who 'becomes revealed'. In Kierkegaard's terminology that means someone who has the strength of mind to face (normal) moral responsibilities (of frankness as well as concern) in spite of certain fundamental obstacles. It is also called 'accomplishing the universal' or 'realizing the universal'. In a version of the legend outlined by Johannes *de silentio* the merman realizes the universal by marrying Agnete, but can only do so 'on the strength of the absurd', by 'making the movement of faith'.

Now Johannes says he understands the merman, because the merman is in the humanly intelligible situation, even the familiar situation, of being prevented by his own guilt from realizing the universal. What is intelligible about this is that the merman has recourse to the absurd (also called the 'paradox') in order to come back to the universal from which guilt has exiled him. But Abraham is not intelligible in this way. For Abraham is already quite capable of accomplishing the universal as far as his obligations to Isaac are concerned. He is and wants always to be a good father to Isaac. What is unintelligible about Abraham is that he is using the paradox to make himself incapable of realizing the universal.

But that is not altogether correct. What Abraham himself would say he was doing, so long as what he says is an expression of his faith, is that he is *retaining* or *reaffirming* his capacity to realize the universal – for after all, his belief, insane though it must seem, is that he is going to get Isaac back even if he sacrifices him. In his faith Abraham does not think he is putting himself outside the universal where the relevant universal is his being able and willing to exercise his fatherly concern for Isaac; what he thinks is that in order to show God his faith he must put the possibility of his continuing to exercise this concern into God's hands. And yet to someone who does not share Abraham's belief in the need to reconstitute the ability to serve the universal on the strength of the absurd, Abraham's action must seem irrational in the extreme. When he already has the capacity to realize the universal, why does he expose himself to what by any rational calculation is the virtual certainty of losing it? That is one aspect of Abraham's irrationality. Another is that Abraham believes he will get Isaac back – but that, according to the text, does have its parallel in the case of the merman, for he too makes the movement of faith 'on the strength of the absurd'. However, there is a third aspect of irrationality that is not shared by the merman. Whereas the merman, so to speak, falls back on this latter irrationality as a (or the only) way of getting back his capacity to accomplish the universal, Abraham can give no better reason for resorting to it than that he must prove his faith to God. So the contrast of intelligibilities as between the merman and Abraham looks something like this (the reader is begged to excuse the complexity of the next few lines, which is due as much to the subject-matter as to my poor ability to express the point more clearly). The fact that the merman resorts to absurdity to regain the capacity to accomplish the universal is partially intelligible, it is intelligible *on the surface*, to someone who equates morality with accomplishment of the universal. But *only* on the surface, because such a person would not understand the element of absurdity and faith that the merman needs in order to re-establish this capacity which a person who makes this equation will unreflectively praise. However, since such a person fails to grasp the means (which in fact imply a subversion of the basis on which he unreflectively finds the merman's goal praiseworthy), he also fails in any genuine way to grasp what it is he is praising the merman for doing. What the merman is genuinely doing is coming back to the universal via a position which no longer equates morality with accomplishment of the universal. As for Abraham, he despite appearances actually has the same kind of aim as the merman. He wants to regain the capacity to accomplish the universal. But for him, since his specific intention is not to accomplish the universal in some particular way but to *prove his faith*, i.e. show that he believes that intentions of the kind the merman genuinely has are the properly moral kind of action, this requires as a means an act of self-incapacitation which no one who equates morality with accomplishment of the universal could ever think of praising, and which such a person could therefore never find intelligible as a moral action. A question that arises here is whether Johannes *de silentio* is intended by Kierkegaard to be such a person, that is someone who superficially understands the merman but because he doesn't understand Abraham doesn't genuinely understand the merman either, or whether we should look further for something that Johannes genuinely understands about the merman but not about Abraham. I leave this question open, though some remarks below indicate the kind of answer that I myself find plausible. The most important conclusion to draw from the above remarks is that the merman and Abraham are engaged in two very different projects. What we are, I think, entitled to conclude from the disanalogy between them is that where the merman is doing one thing, calling on faith to get himself back into the universal (but on another basis than that on which he once belonged to it), Abraham in sacrificing Isaac is doing two: at one level the sacrifice is the act of general resignation that he has to perform before he can show that he believes the goals praised by the 'universalist' can be re-established as praiseworthy on a principle that is the diametrical opposite of that on which the universalist praises them, and at another his ability to carry it through *is* his showing this. Abraham wants to show that the goals can be re-established on the principle that the particular individual is 'higher' than the universal. We should no more take the story of Abraham and Isaac to show us what sort of actions are required for the renunciation that precedes faith in general (let alone, as some claim, that Abraham's action is the kind of thing Kierkegaard means us to expect of moral agents once the individual has got the upper hand and is in direct contact with God), than we should expect the merman's marrying Agnete to be a way of proving his faith to God.

The opening pages of each of the three *problemata* all follow a uniform pattern. First the ethical is defined as the universal, then a consequence drawn from this, followed by the observation that to accept this consequence is to concede that Hegel's account of the ethical is right. Thereupon our author claims that if Hegel's account is indeed right, then Hegelians have no right to talk of faith or to give credit to Abraham as its father, for according to each of the consequences in question Abraham must stand morally (even criminally) condemned. The three consequences of defining the ethical as 'the universal' are: (i) that the individual's moral performance must be judged by its underlying social intention; (ii) that there are no duties to God other than duties that are in the first instance to the universal; and (iii) that it is a moral requirement that one not conceal one's moral projects or the reasons one has for failing to carry them through. In each of the *problemata* Abraham is shown to infringe the principle of the ethical as the universal by failing to conform to the consequence, or implicated requirement, in question. Abraham acts as though there were a superior measure of moral performance that made social intentions irrelevant; he supposes himself to have an absolute duty to God that overrides the ethical defined as the universal; and he cannot reveal his intention to the parties concerned.

The pattern of argument in the *problemata* is thus of the kind logicians call *modus tollens*. The form of such argument is 'If A then B; not-B, therefore not-A'. 'A' may state a general principle or a definition, and B the specified implication of the former. In the case of each of the three specified implications Johannes *de silentio* says quite explicitly that it is also an implication of Hegel's account of ethics. There is good reason to suppose, then, that the principle (or definition) A is intended as a statement of the Hegelian conception of ethics prevailing in Kierkegaard's time. Hegel defined ethical life (Kierkegaard uses a Danish expression, 'det Sædelige', which is a direct translation of Hegel's 'das Sittliche', as the identification of the individual with the totality of his social life.* The basic idea behind an ethics of *Sittlichkeit* is that public morality, or the principles of social and political cohesion underlying any actual society, are expressions of universal human goals. If there is a human *telos* (goal) at all, that is where it finds expression. Thus in order to become moral the individual should conform to, and begin to want to act in accordance with, the principles of public morality that any State must be based on. 'The State', says Hegel, 'in and by itself is the ethical whole.'† This is precisely the idea of the ethical as the universal which the *problemata* present as a hoop that Abraham must jump through in order to prove the morality of his action. Abraham consistently fails. What he himself would say in explanation of his action, that his faith is being put to the test, is quite incomprehensible according to the principle. For on the principle God could only test him by tempting him *out* of his familial and social obligations; there could be no duty to God that was not to be found among those obligations. And worse, Abraham cannot even explain his case, because there is no other way of intelligibly excusing your sacrifice of another as a moral action than by being able to show the one to be sacrificed how the sacrifice in some way contributes to the fulfilment of a social intention higher than that of keeping the person to be sacrificed unharmed. This makes any attempt on Abraham's part to communicate his intention to others a 'temptation': if he can find anything intelligible to say by way of explanation, then he has failed the test, been tempted *by* the ethical (as universal), instead of proving himself to be, as a particular individual, higher than it.

* See 'System der Sittlichkeit', in Hegel's *Schriften zur Politik und Rechtsphilosophie*, Leipzig, 1913. p. 419.
† *Hegel's Philosophy of Right*, trans. T. M. Knox, Oxford University Press, London, 1980. p. 279.

That in brief is the sum of the argument of the *problemata*. It is clear that if Hegel is right then Abraham does teleologically suspend the ethical, he does conceive of an absolute duty to God, and he remains concealed – he *cannot* justify his action to those concerned.

But what is Johannes *de silentio*'s own view? Does he side with Abraham? Or should we rather interpret the *problemata* in a minimal fashion? That is, should we say that all Johannes is doing is to show that *if* you are a Hegelian, *then* you cannot talk glibly of faith as something you have fathomed and can proceed beyond, because according to your principle Abraham is morally evil and a criminal?

This minimal answer leaves open, however, the question of whether Johannes (or Kierkegaard) envisages some alternative principle for morality. I myself believe he (and Kierkegaard) does. But it is one thing to envisage an alternative in the sense simply of not excluding the possibility that there is one, another to envisage it so to speak as present to mind. I would suggest that where Kierkegaard might say that he himself envisaged it in the second sense, Johannes *de silentio* is made to write as if he envisaged it only in the first. The story of Abraham and Isaac indicates only in outline, and by symbolizing its formal features, the view that it is possible for someone to qualify as essentially human independently of any specification one may give of what, in the context of intention and action, is properly human in general. This would be unthinkable to Hegelians. They would assume as a matter of principle that there is an inseparable link between acquiring the status of a developed human being and conforming ever more successfully to, and convergently upon, some accepted general specification of 'human'. What they would never be able to understand in Abraham is that for him it is not any revealed balance of human gain in respect of the total social life of a community that counts for the humanity of an action. Abraham acts as though someone could be properly human prior to the expression of his or her humanity in the universal, so that the universal becomes an expression in turn of a humanity pre-established, as it were, at the level of the particular and no longer the category *in which* humanity is established.*

Where Hegelians believe individuals realize themselves by being taken up, consciously and willingly, in the universal, Abraham represents a diametrically opposite view in which the universal – or the presence of a social intention – has first to be established prior to entering (or re-entering) the universal. Its being formed in the individual is, so Kierkegaard believed his own experience to have taught him, no easy matter; in the end it requires faith, in the sense that Johannes *de silentio* is made to clarify. However, Johannes's platform is still that of his (contemporary) readers. The postulate that the ethical is the universal is one he accepts, at least as the only going ethical principle available to him. And he uses it to test the distance between his sense of the greatness of Abraham and his ability to understand him. Really what he uncovers is the extent of the inability of those who accept the Hegelian principle to understand Abraham. But that is because the readers Kierkegaard has designed him for are wedded to that principle. Kierkegaard's overriding aim is to divorce them from it, but he believes that has to be done with their own consent and therefore with due regard to their own conceptual and attitudinal presuppositions. In a work published after his death Kierkegaard gives some guidelines as to how to interpret his 'aesthetic' and 'dialectical' works. He says the former are to lead the reader to Christian concepts 'back' from the 'aesthetic' way of interpreting them, back from the point of view of the life of immediacy, and the latter 'back' from the System and speculative philosophy. In the case of the aesthetic works his method, he says, is to deceive. In answer to his own question about what the deception amounts to in this case, he says:

> It means that one doesn't begin *directly* with what one wants to communicate, but ... going along with the other's delusion. Thus (to keep to the present work's topic) one begins by saying, not 'I'm a Christian, you are not', but 'You are a Christian, I

* This is stated in some greater detail in my *Kierkegaard*, Routledge & Kegan Paul. London, 1982, esp. pp. 87–8.

am not'. Not by saying 'It is Christianity I preach, and the life
you lead is purely aesthetic [the life of immediacy]', but by saying
'Let's talk about the aesthetic'. The deception is that one does
this precisely in order to come to the religious. But according
to the assumption, the other is also under the delusion that the
aesthetic is the Christian, since he thinks he is a Christian and
yet lives the life [of immediacy].*

At one point in *Fear and Trembling*, where Johannes *de silentio*
says he doesn't understand Abraham, he also says that to understand him we need a new category. This is almost certainly
the Christian concept of faith (not Abraham's) defined and
elaborated at great length in *Philosophical Fragments* and
particularly *Concluding Unscientific Postscript*. Actually the concept of faith developed there helps us in no way to understand
Abraham's willingness to sacrifice Isaac as a 'trial'. What it does
is provide the basis for the alternative ethical paradigm which
Johannes *de silentio* is only able to chart by banging his head
up against the limits of the Hegelian paradigm. That is what
it is his job as a pseudonymous author to do. Johannes *de silentio*
operates 'dialectically' (as he himself says), but only from the
perspective of people who live the life of immediacy. They don't
have the Christian concept of faith and nor does he. The new
paradigm is reserved for later pseudonyms who take on Hegel's
System more directly and whose readers are people who need
to be brought back from that. They too are deluded. They are
'absent-minded' because they have allowed themselves to be
so much swallowed up in the system that they have lost sight
of what it means to exist, of the sense of being a *particular*, and
in the process have given intellectual support to a prevailing
'pantheistically dissolute contempt for individual people'.† They
have to be *humoured* out of their delusion. But that is another
(though not entirely different) story.

*

* *Synspunktet for min Forfatter-Virksomhed: En ligefrem Meddelelse, Rapport til
Historien* (*The Point of View for my Work as an Author: A Direct Communication –
Report to History*), *Samlede Værker*, ed. A. B. Drachmann, J. L. Heiberg, and H.
O. Lange, Copenhagen. Vol. 18 (1964), p. 105.
† *Concluding Unscientific Postscript*, op. cit., p. 317. The translation here is my
own.

Introductions to works of Kierkegaard's usually begin with a summary of his life. I have chosen to put my summary at the end. The reason is that if one puts too much emphasis on the points of biographical relevance that keep on cropping up, particularly in the so-called aesthetic works, one loses sight of the compositional integrity of the best of Kierkegaard's writings. This is undoubtedly true of *Fear and Trembling*, in which almost every page, certainly every illustration, from myth, folk-tale, history, or Kierkegaard's own imagination, bears witness to its actual author's real-life preoccupations at the time.

The work appeared when Søren Aabye Kierkegaard was thirty. It came eight months after the publication of his first main, and much larger, work, *Either/Or: A Fragment of Life*, and thus marks the beginning of a period of intense activity that saw more than a dozen major publications by the year 1850. The background can be briefly sketched. Kierkegaard (an earlier spelling of the Danish for 'churchyard', but carrying as in English the primary connotation of 'graveyard') was born in Copenhagen on 5 May 1813. His father's family had worked the land of their local priest in Jutland, in a feudal arrangement that gave them their name. The father himself had been released from his virtual vassalage by the priest at the age of twenty-one, at a time when he had already moved to Copenhagen to work in an uncle's hosiery business. Kierkegaard senior later became a wealthy wholesaler of imported goods and Søren inherited a fair fortune when his father died. Søren was the youngest of seven children whose mother was their father's second wife and had formerly been maid to the first. A brother and sister died before he was nine. His two surviving sisters, a brother, and his mother all died not long before he was twenty-one, and Søren became convinced that he himself would not live to be more than thirty-three. He was educated at a strictly run School of Civic Virtue, gained there a reputation for a quick tongue and a sharp wit, and then at the University, where he enrolled in 1830. His chosen subject was theology, but he studied liberal arts and science as well, spending in all seven years as a student, his father footing the not inconsiderable bills.

In 1837 he met Regine Olsen, daughter of a Copenhagen

dignitary. Regine was then fourteen years old. The following year Kierkegaard's father died. The father had exercised a great and largely oppressive influence on the son from early childhood, and Kierkegaard eventually found it necessary to try to recapture his spontaneity by breaking himself free. In 1835 he had begun describing Christianity, associated with his father, as a debilitating influence. He looked about him for some other idea 'to live or die for',* forsook his studies, and led outwardly the life of a rich young man about town, aesthete, and wit. Entries in his journal, however, tell a different story. Kierkegaard was really undergoing a period of deep depression, which nevertheless culminated in a reconciliation with his father shortly before the latter's death at the age of eighty-one (Kierkegaard being then twenty-five). Then came the affair with Regine. They became engaged on 10 September 1840 and all seemed set for a life of civic virtue.

But that was not to be. Although in the year following the betrothal he had undergone the necessary practical training for a career in the State Church, and, possibly with an academic career in mind, had begun work on his doctoral thesis, and had even preached his first sermon, in August 1841 he returned Regine's engagement ring. By November of that year, not long after his successful defence of the thesis (*The Concept of Irony with Constant Reference to Socrates*), the break with Regine was final and he was on his way to Berlin, attending Schelling's lectures there (at about the same time, it is thought, as Karl Marx did the same, though there is no record of their meeting). The reasons for this turn of events are not easy to pinpoint, but the crux seems to have been Kierkegaard's sense of his inability to fulfil the personal conditions of a civic life, in particular those involved in being husband and father. Whatever the reasons, there followed the flood of pseudonymous and non-pseudonymous works, beginning in February 1843 with *Either/Or* (in two volumes, each of over 400 pages), followed by *Repetition* and *Fear and Trembling*, and eight months subsequently to these by *Philosophical Fragments* and *The Concept*

---

* The details of Kierkegaard's life are largely gathered from Josiah Thompson's excellent biography, *Kierkegaard*, A. A. Knopf, New York, 1973.

of Anxiety (June 1844). These were relatively slim volumes, but then came the substantial *Stages on Life's Way* followed by the 'dialectical' *Concluding Unscientific Postscript to the Philosophical Fragments*, directed at philosophers of the Hegelian tradition. Alongside this already impressive production Kierkegaard also published twenty-one 'edifying' and 'Christian' discourses under his own name.

Fear and Trembling belongs to the series of works (*Either/Or, Repetition, Stages on Life's Way*) concerned with 'realizing the universal', a theme close to Kierkegaard's heart in view of his decision not to proceed with his marriage. But in *Fear and Trembling* this theme is set in sharp juxtaposition with two others, faith and sacrifice. The relevance of the latter, and thus also the appeal to Kierkegaard of the story of Abraham and Isaac, is obvious enough. In one respect Kierkegaard was sacrificing Regine, who obviously wanted the marriage; in another he was sacrificing himself, since he obviously wanted Regine; and in yet another he perhaps felt that his whole life had been sacrificed through his father (Abraham?), at least ruined as far as being healthily adapted in mind as well as body to accepting the responsibilities and pleasures of family life and a solid job is concerned, and therefore a preparation for some higher mission. As an expert psychologist Kierkegaard was well able to sort out these possible constructions of his situations for himself, and to question the corresponding motives, as well as his own motives for adopting any of them. Thus, to think of the pain he caused Regine as a sacrifice to a higher mission the pain his father had caused him had somehow prepared him, and maybe even specially him, to carry out, could well be a stratagem to conceal some less worthy motive. The ways in which he thought of handling the break with Regine are repeated (from his journals) in the final version he constructs of the legend of Agnete and the merman. So too with faith. In his journals he wrote that if he had had faith – faith for *this* life – he would have stayed with Regine.* But that too would have required sacrifice, at least of his career as a writer and all that his life had seemed to be a preparation for.

* *Søren Kierkegaards Papirer*, Copenhagen, Vol. IV (1968), A 107 and 108.

It was in any case the career of a writer that he pursued until his death at the age of forty-two. By that time (11 November 1855) he had managed to make himself an object of public ridicule by provoking a feud with a satiric weekly, which mercilessly caricatured him, his posture, clothes, and unusual, jerky gait, but also a public nuisance, by launching a sustained and bitter attack on the Danish State Church and its more eminent functionaries. There were further publications, notably *The Sickness unto Death* (1849) and *Practice in Christianity* (1850), a number of 'Christian Discourses', and a broadsheet which Kierkegaard himself published, called *The Instant* (*Øieblikket*). This ran through nine issues before Kierkegaard fell ill, collapsed in the street, and died in hospital some six weeks later, probably of a lung infection. On his sickbed he confided to his friend from boyhood, one Emil Boesen, now a pastor and the only member of the Church he would see, even though his own brother was a clergyman, that his life had been a 'great and to others unknown and incomprehensible suffering' which looked like 'pride and vanity' but 'wasn't'. He regretted that he hadn't married or taken on an official position. Kierkegaard's funeral was the occasion of a minor disturbance led by his student nephew, who protested at the Church's insistence on officiating at the committal proceedings, contrary to the deceased's wishes.

*

In the Preface to *Fear and Trembling* the author sports with the notion of 'going further', an expression I also used at the beginning of this introduction. It was used by H. L. Martensen, Kierkegaard's former tutor at Copenhagen University and later Bishop Primate, in a review where he claimed that one should move forward from the methodological doubt of Descartes to Hegel and even beyond. Kierkegaard uses doubt as a parallel to faith, as something hard enough to get to, let alone to go further than. This is typical of the 'situational' character of most of Kierkegaard's writings. They were written for contemporary readers who, unlike us, would be quick to catch the allusions and identify the references. He wrote in Danish, of course, and could have entertained no expectation that his works would become 'classics'. However, concerning *Fear and Trembling*, he did predict that with its 'frightful pathos' this early work 'alone' would suffice 'to immortalize my name as an author'. Moreover, once he was dead and his reputation for flippancy and wit no longer prevented readers from taking the book seriously, it would 'be read' but also 'translated into other languages' (*Papers and Journals: A Selection*, Harmondsworth, Penguin Books, 1996, p. 425).

FEAR AND TREMBLING

Dialectical Lyric by
Johannes *de silentio*

What Tarquin the Proud said in his garden with the poppy blooms was understood by the son but not by the messenger.
HAMANN[1]

PREFACE

Not just in commerce but in the world of ideas too our age is putting on a veritable clearance sale. Everything can be had so dirt cheap that one begins to wonder whether in the end anyone will want to make a bid. Every speculative score-keeper who conscientiously marks up the momentous march of modern philosophy, every lecturer, crammer, student, everyone on the outskirts of philosophy or at its centre is unwilling to stop with doubting everything. They all go further. It would perhaps be malapropos to inquire where they think they are going, though surely we may in all politeness and respect take it for granted that they have indeed doubted everything, otherwise it would be odd to talk of going further. This preliminary step is one they have all of them taken, and presumably with so little effort as to feel no need to drop some word about how; for not even someone genuinely anxious for a little enlightenment on this will find such. Not a gesture that might point him in the right direction, no small dietary prescription for how to go about such a huge task. 'But Descartes did it, didn't he?' A venerable, humble, honest thinker whose writings surely no one can read without being most deeply stirred – Descartes must have done what he has said and said what he has done. A rare enough occurrence in our own time! Descartes, as he himself repeatedly insists, was no doubter in matters of faith. ('[B]ut we must keep in mind what has been said, that we must trust to this natural light only so long as nothing contrary to it is revealed by God himself ... Above all we should impress on our memory as an infallible rule that what God has revealed to us is incomparably more certain than anything else; and that we ought to submit to the Divine authority rather than to our own judgement even though the light of reason may seem to us to suggest, with the utmost clearness and evidence, something opposite' [from Principles 28 and 76 of *Principles of Philosophy*].[2]) Descartes has not cried 'Fire!' and made it everyone's duty to doubt, for

Descartes was a quiet and lonely thinker, not a bellowing street-watch; he was modest enough to allow that his method was important only for himself and sprang partly from his own earlier bungling with knowledge. ('Thus my design here is not to teach the Method which everyone should follow in order to promote the good conduct of Reason, but only to show in what manner I have endeavoured to conduct my own ... But so soon as I had achieved the entire course of study [that is, of his youth – Johannes *de silentio*'s interpolation] at the close of which one is usually received into the ranks of the learned, I entirely changed my opinion. For I found myself embarrassed with so many doubts and errors that it seemed to me that the effort to instruct myself had no effect other than the increasing discovery of my own ignorance' [*Discourse on the Method of Rightly Conducting the Reason and Seeking the Truth in the Sciences*].[3]) – What those old Greeks, whom one must also credit with a little knowledge of philosophy, took to be the task of a whole lifetime, doubt not being a skill one acquires in days and weeks; what the old veteran warrior achieved after keeping the balance of doubt in the face of all inveiglements, fearlessly rejecting the certainties of sense and thought, incorruptibly defying selfish anxieties and the wheedling of sympathies – that is where nowadays everyone begins.

Today nobody will stop with faith; they all go further. It would perhaps be rash to inquire where to, but surely a mark of urbanity and good breeding on my part to assume that in fact everyone does indeed have faith, otherwise it would be odd to talk of going further. In those old days it was different. For then faith was a task for a whole lifetime, not a skill thought to be acquired in either days or weeks. When the old campaigner approached the end, had fought the good fight,[4] and kept his faith, his heart was still young enough not to have forgotten the fear and trembling that disciplined his youth and which, although the grown man mastered it, no man altogether outgrows – unless he somehow manages at the earliest possible opportunity to go further. Where these venerable figures arrived our own age begins, in order to go further.

The present author is no philosopher, he has not understood

the System, nor does he know if there really is one, or if it has been completed. As far as his own weak head is concerned the thought of what huge heads everyone must have in order to have such huge thoughts is already enough. Even if one were able to render the whole of the content of faith into conceptual form, it would not follow that one had grasped faith, grasped how one came to it, or how it came to one. The present author is no philosopher, he is *poetice et eleganter* [to put it in poetic and well-chosen terms], a freelance who neither writes the System nor makes any *promises* about it, who pledges neither anything about the System nor himself *to* it. He writes because for him doing so is a luxury, the more agreeable and conspicuous the fewer who buy and read what he writes. In an age where passion has been done away with for the sake of science he easily foresees his fate – in an age when an author who wants readers must be careful to write in a way that he can be comfortably leafed through during the after-dinner nap, and be sure to present himself to the world like the polite gardener's boy in the *Advertiser*[5] who, hat in hand and with good references from his previous place of employment, recommends himself to a much-esteemed public. He foresees his fate will be to be completely ignored; has a dreadful foreboding that the scourge of zealous criticism will more than once make itself felt; and shudders at what terrifies him even more, that some enterprising recorder, a paragraph swallower who to rescue learning is always willing to do to others' writings what, to 'preserve good taste', Trop[6] nobly did to *The Destruction of the Human Race*, will slice him into sections as ruthlessly as the man who, in the service of the science of punctuation, divided up his speech by counting the words and putting a full-stop after every fifty and a semi-colon after every thirty-five. No, I prostrate myself before any systematic bag-searcher; this is not the System, it hasn't the slightest thing to do with the System. I wish all good on the System and on the Danish shareholders in that omnibus[7]; for it will hardly become a tower.[8] I wish them good luck and prosperity one and all.

Respectfully
Johannes *de silentio*

ATTUNEMENT

There was once a man; he had learned as a child that beautiful tale of how God tried Abraham, how he withstood the test, kept his faith and for the second time received a son against every expectation. When he became older he read the same story with even greater admiration, for life had divided what had been united in the child's pious simplicity. The older he became the more often his thoughts turned to that tale, his enthusiasm became stronger and stronger, and yet less and less could he understand it. Finally it put everything else out of his mind; his soul had but one wish, actually to see Abraham, and one longing, to have been witness to those events. It was not the beautiful regions of the East, nor the earthly splendour of the Promised Land, he longed to see, not the God-fearing couple whose old age God had blessed, not the venerable figure of the patriarch stricken in years, not the youthful vigour God gave to Isaac – it would have been the same if it had taken place on a barren heath. What he yearned for was to accompany them on the three-day journey, when Abraham rode with grief before him and Isaac by his side. He wanted to be there at that moment when Abraham raised his eyes and saw in the distance the mountain in Moriah, the moment he left the asses behind and went on up the mountain alone with Isaac. For what occupied him was not the finely wrought fabric of imagination, but the shudder of thought.

This man was no thinker, he felt no need to go further than faith. To be remembered as its father seemed to him to be surely the greatest glory of all, and to have it a lot to be envied even if no one else knew.

This man was no learned exegete, he knew no Hebrew; had he known Hebrew then perhaps it might have been easy for him to understand the story of Abraham.

I

And it came to pass after these things, that God did tempt Abraham, and said unto him ... Take now thy son, thine only son Isaac, whom thou lovest, and get thee into the land of Moriah; and offer him there for a burnt offering upon one of the mountains which I will tell thee of.[9]

It was early morning. Abraham rose in good time, had the asses saddled and left his tent, taking Isaac with him, but Sarah watched them from the window as they went down the valley[10] until she could see them no more. They rode in silence for three days; on the morning of the fourth Abraham still said not a word, but raised his eyes and saw afar the mountain in Moriah. He left the lads behind and went on alone up the mountain with Isaac beside him. But Abraham said to himself: 'I won't conceal from Isaac where this way is leading him.' He stood still, laid his hand on Isaac's head to give him his blessing, and Isaac bent down to receive it. And Abraham's expression was fatherly, his gaze gentle, his speech encouraging. But Isaac could not understand him, his soul could not be uplifted; he clung to Abraham's knees, pleaded at his feet, begged for his young life, for his fair promise; he called to mind the joy in Abraham's house, reminded him of the sorrow and loneliness. Then Abraham lifted the boy up and walked with him, taking him by the hand, and his words were full of comfort and exhortation. But Isaac could not understand him. Abraham climbed the mountain in Moriah, but Isaac did not understand him. Then he turned away from Isaac for a moment, but when Isaac saw his face a second time it was changed, his gaze was wild, his mien one of horror. He caught Isaac by the chest, threw him to the ground and said: 'Foolish boy, do you believe I am your father? I am an idolater. Do you believe this is God's command? No, it is my own desire.' Then Isaac trembled and in his anguish cried: 'God in heaven have mercy on me, God of Abraham have mercy on me; if I have no father on earth, then be Thou my father!' But below his breath Abraham said to himself: 'Lord in heaven I thank Thee; it is after all better that he believe I am a monster than that he lose faith in Thee.'

*

When the child is to be weaned the mother blackens her breast, for it would be a shame were the breast to look pleasing when the child is not to have it. So the child believes that the breast has changed but the mother is the same, her look loving and tender as ever. Lucky the one that needed no more terrible means to wean the child!

II

It was early morning. Abraham rose in good time, embraced Sarah, the bride of his old age, and Sarah kissed Isaac, who had taken her disgrace from her, was her pride and hope for all generations. So they rode on in silence and Abraham's eyes were fixed on the ground, until the fourth day when he looked up and saw afar the mountain in Moriah, but he turned his gaze once again to the ground. Silently he arranged the firewood, bound Isaac; silently he drew the knife. Then he saw the ram that God had appointed. He sacrificed that and returned home ... From that day on, Abraham became old, he could not forget that God had demanded this of him. Isaac throve as before; but Abraham's eye was darkened, he saw joy no more.

*

When the child has grown and is to be weaned the mother virginally covers her breast, so the child no more has a mother. Lucky the child that lost its mother in no other way!

III

It was early morning. Abraham rose in good time, kissed Sarah the young mother, and Sarah kissed Isaac, her delight, her joy for ever. And Abraham rode thoughtfully on. He thought of Hagar and of the son whom he had driven out into the desert. He climbed the mountain in Moriah, he drew the knife.

It was a tranquil evening when Abraham rode out alone, and he rode to the mountain in Moriah; he threw himself on his face, he begged God to forgive his sin at having been willing to sacrifice Isaac, at the father's having forgotten his duty to his son. He rode more frequently on his lonely way, but found no peace. He could not comprehend that it was a sin to have been willing to sacrifice to God the best he owned; that for which he would many a time have gladly laid down his own life; and if it was a sin, if he had not so loved Isaac, then he could not understand that it could be forgiven; for what sin was more terrible?

*

When the child is to be weaned the mother too is not without sorrow, that she and the child grow more and more apart; that the child which first lay beneath her heart, yet later rested at her breast, should no longer be so close. Thus together they suffer this brief sorrow. Lucky the one who kept the child so close and had no need to sorrow more!

IV

It was early morning. Everything had been made ready for the journey in Abraham's house. Abraham took leave of Sarah, and the faithful servant Eliezer followed him out on the way until he had to turn back. They rode together in accord, Abraham and Isaac, until they came to the mountain in Moriah. Yet Abraham made everything ready for the sacrifice, calmly and quietly, but as he turned away Isaac saw that Abraham's left hand was clenched in anguish, that a shudder went through his body – but Abraham drew the knife.

Then they turned home again and Sarah ran to meet them, but Isaac had lost his faith. Never a word in the whole world

is spoken of this,[11] and Isaac told no one what he had seen,
and Abraham never suspected that anyone had seen it.

*

When the child is to be weaned the mother has more solid
food at hand, so that the child will not perish. Lucky the one who
has more solid food at hand!

In these and similar ways this man of whom we speak thought
about those events. Every time he came home from a journey
to the mountain in Moriah he collapsed in weariness, clasped
his hands, and said: 'Yet no one was as great as Abraham; who
is able to understand him?'

SPEECH IN PRAISE OF ABRAHAM

If there were no eternal consciousness in a man, if at the bottom of everything there were only a wild ferment, a power that twisting in dark passions produced everything great or inconsequential; if an unfathomable, insatiable emptiness lay hid beneath everything, what then would life be but despair? If it were thus, if there were no sacred bond uniting mankind, if one generation rose up after another like the leaves of the forest,[12] if one generation succeeded the other as the songs of birds in the woods, if the human race passed through the world as a ship through the sea or the wind through the desert, a thoughtless and fruitless whim, if an eternal oblivion always lurked hungrily for its prey and there were no power strong enough to wrest it from its clutches – how empty and devoid of comfort would life be! But for that reason it is not so, and as God created man and woman, so too he shaped the hero and the poet or speech-maker. The latter has none of the skills of the former, he can only admire, love, take pleasure in the hero. Yet he, too, no less than the hero, is happy; for the hero is so to speak that better nature of his in which he is enamoured, though happy that it is not himself, that his love can indeed be admiration. He is the spirit of remembrance, can only bring to mind what has been done, do nothing but admire what has been done. He takes nothing of himself, but is jealous of his charge. He follows his heart's desire, but having found what he sought he wanders round in front of everyone's door with his song and his speech, so that all can admire the hero as he does, be proud of the hero as he is. That is his achievement, his humble task, this his faithful service in the hero's house. If he remains thus true to his love, if he struggles night and day against the wiles of oblivion, which would cheat him of his hero, then he has fulfilled his task, he is united with the hero who in his turn has loved him just as faithfully, for the poet is so to speak the *hero's* better nature, ineffectual certainly as a memory is, but also transfigured as a memory is. Therefore no one who was great will be forgotten: and however long it takes, even if a cloud of misunderstanding[13] should take the hero away, his lover still comes, and the more time goes by the more faithfully he sticks by him.

No! No one shall be forgotten who was great in this world; but everyone was great in his own way, and everyone in proportion to the greatness of what *he loved*. For he who loved himself became great in himself, and he who loved others became great through his devotion, but he who loved God became greater than all. They shall all be remembered, but everyone became great in proportion to his *expectancy*. One became great through expecting the possible, another by expecting the eternal; but he who expected the impossible became greater than all. They shall all be remembered, but everyone was great in proportion to the magnitude of what he *strove with*. For he who strove with the world became great by conquering the world, and he who strove with himself became greater by conquering himself; but he who strove with God became greater than all. Thus there was strife in the world, man against man, one against thousands, but he who strove with God was greater than all. Thus there was strife upon earth: there was he who conquered everything by his own strength, and he who conquered God by his powerlessness. There was one who relied upon himself and gained everything, and one who, secure in his own strength, sacrificed everything; but greater than all was the one who believed God. There was one who was great in his strength, and one who was great in his wisdom, and one who was great in hope, and one who was great in love; but greater than all was Abraham, great with that power whose strength is powerlessness, great in that wisdom whose secret is folly,[14] great in that hope whose outward form is insanity, great in that love which is hatred of self.

It was by his faith that Abraham could leave the land of his fathers to become a stranger in the land of promise.[15] He left one thing behind, took another with him. He left behind his worldly understanding and took with him his faith. Otherwise he would surely not have gone; certainly it would have been senseless to do so. It was by his faith that he could be a stranger in the promised land; there was nothing to remind him of what was dear, but the novelty of everything tempted his soul to sad longing. And yet he was God's chosen, in whom the Lord was well pleased! Yes, indeed! If only he had been disowned, cast out from God's grace, he would have understood it better. As it was it looked more like a mockery of himself and his faith. There was once another who lived in exile from the beloved land of his fathers.[16] He is not forgotten, nor his songs of lament in which in sorrow he sought and found what he had lost. From Abraham we have no song of lament. It is human to complain, human to weep with one who weeps, but it is greater to have faith and more blessed to behold the believer.

It was faith that made Abraham accept the promise that all nations of the earth should be blessed in his seed.[17] Time went by, the possibility was still there, and Abraham had faith; time went by, it became unlikely, and Abraham had faith. There was once another who held out an expectation. Time went by, the evening drew near, he was not so pitiful as to forget his expectation; therefore he too should not be forgotten. Then he sorrowed, and the sorrow did not deceive him as life had done; it did all it could for him and in the sweetness of sorrow he possessed his disappointed expectation. It is human to sorrow with the sorrower, but greater to have faith and more blessed to behold the believer. From Abraham we have no song of sorrow. As time went by he did not mournfully count the days, he did not cast suspicious glances at Sarah, fearing she was growing old; he did not stay the march of the sun[18] so that Sarah should not grow old and with her his expectation; he did not soothingly sing to Sarah his mournful lay. Abraham became old and Sarah was mocked in the land, and still he was God's chosen and heir to the promise that in his seed all nations of the earth would be blessed. Would it not be better, then, were he not God's chosen? What is it to be God's chosen? Is it to be denied in youth one's youthful desire in order to have it fulfilled in great travail in old age? But Abraham believed and held firm to the promise. Had Abraham wavered he would have renounced it. He would have said to God: 'So perhaps after all

it is not your will that it should happen; then I will give-up
my desire, it was my only desire, my blessed joy. My soul is
upright, I bear no secret grudge because you refused it.' He
would not have been forgotten, he would have saved many
by his example, yet he would not have become the father of
faith; for it is great to give up one's desire, but greater to
stick to it after having given it up; it is great to grasp hold of
the eternal but greater to stick to the temporal after having
given it up. But then came the fullness of time. Had Abraham
not had faith, then Sarah would surely have died of sorrow,
and Abraham, dull with grief, instead of understanding the
fulfilment, would have smiled at it as at a youthful dream. But
Abraham believed, and therefore he *was* young; for he who
always hopes for the best becomes old, deceived by life, and he
who is always prepared for the worst becomes old prematurely;
but he who has faith, retains eternal youth. All praise then
to that tale! For Sarah, though stricken in years, was young
enough to covet the pleasure of motherhood; and Abraham,
though grey of head, was young enough to want to be a
father. Outwardly the wonder of faith is in Abraham and
Sarah's being young enough for it to happen according to their
expectations; in a deeper sense the wonder of faith lies in
Abraham and Sarah's being young enough to wish, and in
faith's having preserved their wish and through it their youth-
fulness. He accepted the fulfilment of the promise, he accepted
it in faith, and it happened according to expectation and according to faith; for Moses struck the rock with his rod[19] but he did
not believe.

So there was rejoicing in Abraham's house when Sarah was
bride on their golden-wedding day.

But it was not to remain so; Abraham was to be tried once
more. He had fought with that subtle power that invents everything, with that watchful opponent that never takes a nap, with
that old man who outlives everything – time itself. He had fought
with it and kept his faith. Now all the horrors of the struggle
were to be concentrated in one moment. 'And God did tempt
Abraham, and said unto him ... Take now thy son, thine only
son Isaac, whom thou lovest, and get thee into the land of

Moriah; and offer him there for a burnt offering upon one of the mountains which I will tell thee of.'

So all was lost, more terrible than if it had never been! So the Lord was only making sport of Abraham! Through a miracle he had made the preposterous come true, now he would see it again brought to nothing. Foolery indeed! But Abraham did not laugh at it, as Sarah had laughed when the promise had first been proclaimed.[20] All was lost! Seventy years' faithful expectation, the brief joy at faith's fulfilment.[21] Who is it then that snatches the staff from the old man, who is it that demands that the old man himself should break it? Who is it that makes a man's grey hairs forlorn, who is it that demands that he himself should make them so? Is there no compassion for this venerable greybeard, none for the innocent child? And yet Abraham was God's chosen, and it was the Lord who put him to this test. All was now surely lost! The glorious memory of the human race, the promise in Abraham's seed,[22] it was only a whim, a fleeting thought of the Lord's, which Abraham himself must now eradicate. That glorious treasure, as old as the faith in Abraham's heart, many many years older than Isaac, the fruit of Abraham's life, hallowed with prayers, ripened in struggle – the blessing on Abraham's lips, this fruit was now to be plucked out of season and have no meaning; for what meaning could there be in it if Isaac was to be sacrificed! That sad yet still blessed hour when Abraham should take leave of everything he held dear, when he should raise his venerable head one time more, when his countenance should be radiant as the Lord's, when he should concentrate his whole soul in a blessing with the power to give Isaac joy all his days – that moment was not to come! For, yes, Abraham would indeed take leave of Isaac, but it was he that was to remain; death would divide them, but Isaac was to be its victim. The old man was not to lay his hand upon Isaac in blessing, but weary of life was to lay it upon him in violence. And it was God who tried him. Yes. Woe, woe to the messenger who came before Abraham with such tidings! Who would have dared be the emissary of such sorrow? Yet it was God who tried Abraham.

But Abraham had faith, and had faith for *this* life. Yes, had his faith only been for a future life it would indeed have been easier to cast everything aside in order to hasten out of this world to which he did not belong. But Abraham's faith was not of that kind, if there is such, for a faith like that is not really faith but only its remotest possibility, a faith that has some inkling of its object at the very edge of the field of vision but remains separated from it by a yawning abyss in which despair plays its pranks. But it was for this life that Abraham believed, he believed he would become old in his land, honoured among his people, blessed in his kin, eternally remembered in Isaac, the dearest in his life, whom he embraced with a love for which it was but a poor expression to say that he faithfully fulfilled the father's duty to love the son, as indeed the summons put it: 'the son whom thou lovest.' Jacob had twelve sons and he loved one; Abraham had just one, the son he loved.

But Abraham had faith and did not doubt. He believed the absurd. If Abraham had doubted – then he would have done something else, something great and glorious; for how could Abraham have done other than what is great and glorious? He would have marched out to the mountain in Moriah, chopped the firewood, set light to the fire, drawn the knife – he would have cried out to God: 'Do not scorn this sacrifice, it is not the best I possess, that I well know; for what is an old man compared with the child of promise, but it is the best I can give. Let Isaac never come to know, that he may comfort himself in his young years.' He would have thrust the knife into his own breast. He would have been admired in the world and his name never forgotten; but it is one thing to be admired, another to be a guiding star that saves the anguished.

But Abraham had faith. He did not beg for himself in hope of moving the Lord; it was only that time when the just punishment had been proclaimed upon Sodom and Gomorrah that Abraham came forward with his prayers.[23]

We read in those Holy Scriptures: 'And God did tempt Abraham, and said unto him, Abraham: Abraham, where are you? but Abraham answered: here I am.'[24] You, to whom my speech is addressed, was that the case with you? When you saw, far off, the heavy fate approaching, did you not say to the

mountains, 'hide me', to the hills, 'fall on me'?[25] Or if you were
stronger, did your feet nevertheless not drag along the way?
Did they not hanker, as it were, to get back into the old tracks?
When you were called, did you answer, or did you not? Perhaps
softly and in a whisper? Not so Abraham, gladly, boldly,
trustingly he answered out loud 'here I am'. We read further:
'And Abraham rose up early in the morning.'[26] He hurried as
though to some celebration, and he was at the appointed place,
the mountain in Moriah, early in the morning. He said nothing
to Sarah, nothing to Eliezer. After all, who could have understood him? Hadn't the test by its very nature exacted an oath
of silence from him? 'And [he] clave the wood, he bound Isaac,
he kindled the fire, he drew the knife.' My hearer! Many a father
has felt the loss of his child as the loss of the dearest thing he
has in the world, to be bereft of every hope for the future; yet
no son was the child of promise in the sense that Isaac was
for Abraham. Many a father has lost his child, but then it was
God, the unchangeable and inscrutable will of the Almighty,
it was his hand that took it. Not so with Abraham. For him
a harder trial was reserved; along with the knife the fate of Isaac
was put into Abraham's own hand. And he stood there, the
old man with his only hope! But he did not doubt, he did not
look in anguish to left or right, he did not challenge heaven
with his prayers. He knew it was God the Almighty that tried
him, he knew it was the hardest sacrifice that could be demanded
of him; but he also knew that no sacrifice was too hard when
God demanded it – and he drew the knife.

Who gave strength to Abraham's arm, who kept his right
arm raised so that it did not fall helplessly down! Anyone who
saw this would be paralysed. Who gave strength to Abraham's
soul, so that his eye did not become too clouded to see either
Isaac or the ram! Anyone who saw this would become blind.
And yet rare enough though they may be, those who are both
paralysed and blind, still more rare is he who can tell the story
and give it its due. We know it, all of us – it was only a
trial.

Had Abraham doubted as he stood on the mountain in
Moriah, had he looked about in indecision, if before drawing

the knife he had accidentally caught sight of the ram and God
had allowed him to offer it in place of Isaac – then he would
have gone home, everything would have been as before, he
would have had Sarah, he would have kept Isaac, and yet how
changed! For his withdrawal would have been a flight, his
deliverance an accident, his reward dishonour, his future
perhaps damnation. Then he would have borne witness, not
to his faith or to God's mercy, but to how dreadful was the
journey to the mountain in Moriah. Abraham would not be
forgotten, nor the mountain. Yet it would not be mentioned
like Ararat, where the Ark came to land,[28] but as a horror, for
it was here that Abraham doubted.

Venerable Father Abraham! When you journeyed home from
the mountain in Moriah you needed no speech of praise to
console you for what was lost; for in fact you gained everything
and kept Isaac. Was it not so? The Lord never again took him
from you, you sat happily at table with him in your tent, as
you do in the hereafter in all eternity. Venerable Father
Abraham! Thousands of years have slipped by since those days,
but you need no late-coming lover to snatch your memory from
the power of oblivion; for every mother-tongue commemorates
you – and still you reward your lover more gloriously than anyone. You make him blessed hereafter in your bosom, you
captivate his eye and his heart in the here and now with the
marvel of your deed. Venerable Father Abraham! Second father
to the human race! You who first saw and bore witness to that
tremendous passion that scorns the fearful struggle with the
raging elements and the forces of creation in order to struggle
with God instead, you who first knew that supreme passion,
the sacred, pure, and humble expression of the divine madness
which the pagans admired[29] – forgive him who would speak
in your praise if he did not do it correctly. He spoke humbly,
seeing it is his heart's desire; he spoke briefly, as is fitting; but
he will never forget that you needed a hundred years to get
the son of your old age, against every expectation, that you had
to draw the knife before keeping Isaac; he will never forget that
in one hundred and thirty years you got no further than faith.

PROBLEMATA

* * *

PREAMBLE FROM THE HEART

An old proverb pertaining to the outward and visible world says: 'Only one who works gets bread.'[30] Oddly enough, the saying doesn't apply in the world to which it most properly belongs, for the outward world is subject to the law of imperfection; there it happens time and again that one who gets bread is one who does not work, that one who sleeps gets it in greater abundance than one who labours. In the outward world everything belongs to whoever has it, the outward world is subject to the law of indifference and the genie of the ring obeys the one who wears it, whether he be a Noureddin or an Aladdin,[31] and whoever holds the world's treasures does so however he came by them. It is otherwise in the world of spirit. Here there prevails an eternal divine order, here it does not rain on the just and the unjust alike, here the sun does not shine on both good and evil, here only one who works gets bread, and only one who knows anguish finds rest, only one who descends to the underworld saves the loved one, only one who draws the knife gets Isaac. He who will not work does not get bread, but will be deluded, as the gods deluded Orpheus[32] with an airy figure in place of the beloved, deluded him because he was tender-hearted, not courageous, deluded him because he was a lyre-player, not a man.

Here it is no help to have Abraham as one's father,[33] or seventeen centuries of noble ancestry; of anyone who will not work here one can say what is written about Israel's virgins,[34] he gives birth to wind – while the one who works will give birth to his own father.

Conventional wisdom aims presumptuously to introduce into the world of spirit that same law of indifference under which

the outside world groans. It believes it is enough to have
knowledge of large truths. No other work is necessary. But then
it does not get bread, it starves to death while everything is
transformed into gold. And what else does it know? There were
many thousands in the Greece of the time, countless others in
later generations, who knew all the victories of Miltiades, but
there was only one who lost sleep over them.[35] There were
countless generations that knew the story of Abraham by heart,
word for word. How many did it make sleepless?

Now the story of Abraham has the remarkable quality that
it will always be glorious no matter how impoverished our
understanding of it, but only – for it is true here too – if we
are willing to 'labour and be heavy laden'.[36] But labour they
will not, and yet they still want to understand the story. One
speaks in Abraham's honour, but how? By making it a common-
place: 'his greatness was that he so loved God that he was willing
to offer him the best he had.' That is very true, but 'best' is
a vague expression. In word and thought one can quite safely
identify Isaac with the best, and the man who so thinks can
very well puff at his pipe as he does so, and the listener can
very well leisurely stretch out his legs. If the rich young man
whom Christ met on the road had sold all his possessions and
given them to the poor,[37] we would praise him as we praise
all great deeds, but we would not understand even him without
some labour. Yet he would not have become an Abraham even
had he given away the best he had. What is left out of the
Abraham story is the anguish; for while I am under no obligation
to money, to a son the father has the highest and most sacred
of obligations. Yet anguish is a dangerous affair for the
squeamish, so people forget it, notwithstanding they want to
talk about Abraham. So they talk and in the course of con-
versation they interchange the words 'Isaac' and 'best'. Everything goes excellently. Should someone in the audience be
suffering from insomnia, however, there is likely to be the most
appalling, most profound, tragi-comic misunderstanding. He
goes home, he wants to do just like Abraham; for the son is
certainly the best thing he has. Should that speaker hear word
of this, he might go to the man, summon all his clerical

authority, and shout: 'Loathsome man, dregs of society, what
devil has so possessed you that you wanted to murder your own
son?' And this priest, who had felt no signs of heat or perspiration
while preaching about Abraham, would be surprised at the
righteous wrath with which he fulminates against that poor
man; he would be pleased with himself, for never had he spoken
with such pungency and fervour before. He would say to himself,
and his wife: 'I'm an orator, all I've needed was the opportunity;
when I spoke about Abraham on Sunday I didn't feel at all
carried away.' If the same speaker still had some slight excess
of wit to spare he would surely lose it were the sinner to reply
coolly and with dignity: 'It was in fact what you yourself
preached on Sunday.' How could a priest get such an idea into
his head? And yet he did so, and the mistake was only that
he hadn't known what he was saying. Why doesn't some poet
take up situations like these instead of the stuff and nonsense
that fills comedies and novels? The comic and the tragic con-
verge on each other here in absolute infinity. The priest's speech
was no doubt laughable enough in itself, but became infinitely
more so in its consequence, and yet that was quite natural. Or
suppose the sinner had acceded without protest to the priest's
reprimand; or that zealous cleric had gone happily home, happy
in the knowledge that his effectiveness was not confined to the
pulpit but was above all evident in the irresistible power of his
ministry to souls, inspiring the congregation on Sunday while
on Monday, like a cherub with flaming sword, confronting him
who by his deed would put that old proverb to shame which
says that the world never practices what the priest preaches.*

Should the sinner, on the other hand, not be convinced, his
situation would be tragic enough. He would no doubt be
executed or sent to the madhouse; in short he would have come
into an unhappy relation to so-called reality, though in another
sense I should think that Abraham made him happy; for he
who labours does not perish.

* In olden days people said, 'What a shame things in the world don't go in
the way the priest preaches.' But the time may be coming, not least with the
help of philosophy, when we shall be able to say, 'How fortunate that things
in the world don't go in the way the priest preaches, since at least there's a little
meaning to life, but none in his sermon.'

What explains a contradiction like this speaker's? Is it because Abraham has acquired proprietary rights to the title of great man, so that whatever he does is great, and if anyone else does the same it is a sin, a crying sin? If so, I have no wish to take part in such mindless praise. If faith cannot make it into a holy deed to murder one's own son, then let the judgement fall on Abraham as on anyone else. If one hasn't the courage to think this thought through, to say that Abraham was a murderer, then surely it is better to acquire that courage than to waste time on undeserved speeches in his praise. The ethical expression for what Abraham did is that he was willing to murder Isaac; the religious expression is that he was willing to sacrifice Isaac; but in this contradiction lies the very anguish that can indeed make one sleepless; and yet without that anguish Abraham is not the one he is. Or perhaps Abraham simply didn't do what the story says, perhaps in the context of his times what he did was something quite different. Then let's forget him, for why bother remembering a past that cannot be made into a present? Or perhaps something to do with the ethical aspect slipped that speaker's mind, the fact that Isaac was the son. For if you simply remove faith as a nix and nought there remains only the raw fact that Abraham was willing to murder Isaac, which is easy enough for anyone without faith to imitate; without the faith, that is, which makes it hard.

For my own part I don't lack the courage to think a thought whole. No thought has frightened me so far. Should I ever come across one I hope I will at least have the honesty to say: 'This thought scares me, it stirs up something else in me so that I don't want to think it.' If that is wrong of me I'll no doubt get my punishment. If I had conceded the truth of the judgement that Abraham was a murderer, I am not sure that I would have been able to silence my reverence of him. But if that is what I myself thought, then I would presumably keep quiet, for thoughts like that are not to be intimated to others. However, Abraham is no illusion; he hasn't slept himself to fame; he does not owe his celebrity to any whim of fate.

Can one speak unreservedly of Abraham, then, without risking that someone will go off the rails and do likewise? Unless

I dare to speak quite openly I will simply keep quiet about Abraham, and above all not diminish him so that by that very fact he becomes a snare for the weak. If one makes faith the main thing – that is, makes it what it is – then I imagine one might dare speak of it without that risk in this day of ours which can hardly be said to outdo itself in faith, and it is only in respect of faith that one achieves resemblance to Abraham, not murder. If one makes love into a fleeting mood, into a pleasurable agitation in a person, then one lays traps for the weak when talking of the achievements of love. Of course everyone has momentary feelings, but if those were to be used as reasons for doing the terrible things that love has hallowed as immortal deeds everything would be lost, both the achievement and those misled in this way.

It should be all right, then, to speak about Abraham. The great can never do harm when grasped in their greatness. It is like a two-edged sword, bringing death and salvation. If it should fall to my lot to speak of him, I would begin by showing what a devout and God-fearing man Abraham was, deserving to be called God's chosen. Only such a person is subjected to such a trial; but who is such a person? Next I would describe how Abraham loved Isaac. To that end I would beg the support of all good spirits in making my speech as fervent as is the love of a father for his son. I would hope to describe it in such a way that not many a father in the realm would dare maintain that he loved his son thus. Yet if he did not love as Abraham, all thought of offering Isaac would be a temptation. Here we already have plenty to speak of for several Sundays, so there is no need to rush. The result, if the speech does justice to the theme, will be that some fathers will simply not want to hear more, but be happy for the time being if they have really succeeded in loving as Abraham did. Should one of them after having caught the greatness of Abraham's deed, but also the appallingness of it, venture out on the road, I would saddle my horse and ride along with him. At every stop before we came to the mountain in Moriah I would explain to him that he could still turn back, could rue the misunderstanding that he was called to be tried in a conflict of this nature, could confess that he lacked the courage.

so that if God wanted Isaac God must take him himself. It is my conviction that such a person will not be disavowed, but can be blessed along with all others, though not in time. Even in times of faith would such a person not be judged in this way? I knew someone who once could have saved my life had he possessed magnanimity.[38] He said plainly: 'I see well enough what I could do, but I don't dare. I'm afraid that later I shall lack strength, that I shall regret it.' He was not magnanimous, but would anyone cease to love him on that account?

Having spoken thus, and moved my audience so that they appreciated at least something of the dialectical struggle of faith and its gigantic passion, I would not be guilty of the error they might impute to me by thinking: 'Well, he has faith in such a high degree it's enough for us just to hold on to his coat-tails.' For I would add: 'By no means have I faith. I am a shrewd fellow by nature, such as always have great difficulty making the movement of faith, though I wouldn't attach *any importance in itself to a difficulty which, by overcoming it, brings a shrewd fellow no further than the most ordinary and simple-minded person has already reached without the difficulty.*'

Love, after all, has its priests in the poets, and occasionally one hears a voice that knows how to keep it in shape; but about faith one hears not a word, who speaks in *this* passion's praises? Philosophy goes further. Theology sits all painted at the window courting philosophy's favour, offering philosophy its delights. It is said to be hard to understand Hegel, while understanding Abraham, why, that's a bagatelle. To go beyond Hegel, that is a miracle, but to go beyond Abraham is the simplest of all. I for my part have devoted considerable time to understanding the Hegelian philosophy, believe also that I have more or less understood it, am rash enough to believe that at those points where, despite the trouble taken, I cannot understand it, the reason is that Hegel himself hasn't been altogether clear. All this I do easily, naturally, without it causing me any mental strain. But when I have to think about Abraham I am virtually annihilated. I am all the time aware of that monstrous paradox that is the content of Abraham's life, I am constantly repulsed, and my thought, for all its passion, is unable to enter into it, cannot come one hairbreadth further. I strain every muscle to catch sight of it, but the same instant I become paralysed.

I am not unacquainted with what has been admired as great and magnanimous in the world; my soul feels an affinity with it, and is in all humility convinced that it was in my cause too that the hero strove; as I contemplate his striving I exclaim to myself: *'Jam tua res agitur'* [Now it's your affair that's at stake].³⁹ The hero I can *think* myself *into*, but not Abraham; when I reach that height I fall down since what I'm offered is a paradox. Yet I by no means think that faith is therefore something inferior, on the contrary that it is the highest, at the same time believing it dishonest of philosophy to offer something else instead and to slight faith. Philosophy cannot and should not give us an account of faith, but should understand itself and know just what it has indeed to offer, without taking anything away, least of all cheating people out of something by making them think it is nothing. I am not unacquainted with life's needs and dangers, I do not fear them, and I go to meet them undaunted. I am not unfamiliar with horror, my memory is a faithful wife and my imagination, unlike myself, a diligent maid who sits quietly all day at her work and in the evening can speak so prettily for me that I just have to look at it even if it isn't always landscapes or flowers or pastoral idylls she paints. I have seen horror face to face, I do not flee it in fear but know very well that, however bravely I face it, my courage is not that of faith and not at all to be compared with it. I cannot close my eyes and hurl myself trustingly into the absurd, for me it is impossible, but I do not praise myself on that account. I am convinced that God is love; this thought has for me a pristine lyrical validity. When it is present to me I am unspeakably happy, when it is absent I yearn for it more intensely than the lover for the beloved; but I do not have faith; this courage I lack. God's love is for me, both in a direct and inverse sense, incommensurable with the whole of reality. I am not coward enough to whimper and moan on that account, but neither am I underhand enough to deny that faith is something far higher. I can very well carry on living in my manner, I am happy and satisfied, but my happiness is not that of faith and compared with that is indeed un-

happy. I do not burden God with my petty cares, details don't
concern me, I gaze only upon my love and keep its virginal
flame pure and clear; faith is convinced that God troubles himself
about the smallest thing. In this life I am content to be wedded
to the left hand, faith is humble enough to demand the right;
and that it is indeed humility I don't, and shall never, deny.

But I wonder whether all my contemporaries really are
capable of making the movement of faith? Unless I am much
mistaken they are more inclined to pride themselves for doing
what they don't even think me capable of, i.e. the imperfect.
It is against my nature to do what people so often do, talk
inhumanly about the great as though some thousands of years
were a huge distance; I prefer to talk about it humanly as though
it happened yesterday and let only the greatness itself be the
distance that either exalts or condemns. If – *in the guise of tragic
hero*, for higher than that I cannot come – I were summoned
to such an extraordinary royal progress as that to the mountain
in Moriah I know very well what I would have done. I would
not have been coward enough to stay at home, nor would I
have rested on the way or dawdled, or forgotten the knife to
create some delay; I am fairly certain I would have been there
on the dot, with everything arranged – I might even have come
too early instead, so as to have done with it quickly. But I also
know what else I would have done. The moment I mounted
the horse I would have said to myself: 'Now everything is lost,
God demands Isaac, I sacrifice him, and with him all my joy
– yet God is love and for me continues to be so.' For in the
temporal world God and I cannot talk together, we have no
common language. Perhaps someone or other in our time would
be foolish enough, envious enough of the great, to want to
suppose, and have me suppose, that had I actually done this
I would have done something even greater than Abraham, for
wouldn't my immense resignation be far more idealistic and
poetic than Abraham's narrow-mindedness? And yet this is
the greatest falsehood, for my immense resignation would be
a substitute for faith. Nor could I have made more than the
infinite movement in order to find myself again and rest once
more in myself. Neither would I have loved Isaac as Abraham

did. The fact that I made the movement resolutely might demonstrate my courage humanly speaking, that I loved him with all my soul is a precondition without which the whole affair becomes an act of wickedness, and yet I would not have loved as Abraham loved; for then I would have held back at the very last minute, though without this meaning that I'd arrive late at the mountain in Moriah. Furthermore my behaviour would have vitiated the whole story, for I would have been at a loss had I got Isaac back again. What Abraham found the easiest of all would for me be hard, to find joy again in Isaac! For he who with all the infinity of his soul, *proprio motu et propriis auspiciis* [on his own accord and on his own responsibility], has made the infinite movement and can do no more, that person only keeps Isaac with pain.

But what did Abraham do? He came neither too *early* nor too late. He mounted the ass, he rode slowly down the path. All along he had faith, he believed that God would not demand Isaac of him, while still he was willing to offer him if that was indeed what was demanded. He believed on the strength of the absurd, for there could be no question of human calculation, and it was indeed absurd that God who demanded this of him should in the next instant withdraw the demand. He climbed the mountain, even in that moment when the knife gleamed he believed – that God would not demand Isaac. Certainly he was surprised by the outcome, but by means of a double movement he had come back to his original position and therefore received Isaac more joyfully than the first time. Let us go further. We let Isaac actually be sacrificed. Abraham had faith. His faith was not that he should be happy sometime in the hereafter, but that he should find blessed happiness here in this world. God could give him a new Isaac, bring the sacrificial offer back to life. He believed on the strength of the absurd, for all human calculation had long since been suspended. That sorrow can make one demented may be granted and is hard enough; that there is a strength of will that hauls close enough to the wind to save the understanding, even if the strain turns one slightly odd, that too may be granted. I don't mean to decry that. But to be able to lose one's understanding and with it the whole of the finite world whose stockbroker it is, and then on the strength of the absurd get exactly the same finitude back again, that leaves me aghast. But I don't say on that account that it is of little worth; on the contrary it is the one and only marvel. It is commonly supposed that what faith produces is no work of art but a crude and vulgar effort only for clumsier natures; yet the truth is quite otherwise. The dialectic of faith is the most refined and most remarkable of all dialectics, it has an elevation that I can form a conception of but no more. I can make the great trampoline leap in which I pass over into infinitude, my back is like the tight-rope walker's, twisted in my childhood,[40] and so it is easy for me. One, two, three, I can go upside down in existence, but the next is beyond me, for the marvel I cannot perform but only be amazed at. Yes, if only Abraham, the instant he swung his leg over the ass's back, had said to himself: 'Now Isaac is lost, I could just as well sacrifice him here at home as journey the long road to Moriah' – then I wouldn't need Abraham, whereas now I bow to his name seven times and to his deed seventy.[41] For that is not what he did, as I can prove by the fact that he received Isaac back with joy, really heartfelt joy, that he needed no preparation, no time to adjust himself to finitude and its joy. Had it not been thus with Abraham he may well have loved God, but he would not have had faith; for he who loves God without faith reflects on himself, while the person who loves God in faith reflects on God.

At this extremity stands Abraham. The last stage he loses sight of is infinite resignation. He really does go further and comes *to* faith, for all these caricatures of faith, the pitiable, lukewarm apathy that thinks 'There's surely no need, it's not worth worrying before the time', the miserable hope that says 'Who knows what may happen, it's possible certainly' – these distortions belong to life's wretchedness, and these infinite resignation has already infinitely scorned.

Abraham I cannot understand; in a way all I can learn from him is to be amazed. If one imagines one can be moved to faith by considering the outcome of this story, one deceives oneself, and is out to cheat God of faith's first movement, one is out to suck the life-wisdom out of the paradox. One or another may succeed, for our age does not stop with faith, with its miracle of turning water into wine;[42] it goes further, it turns wine into water.

Would it not be best all the same to stop with faith, and is it not disturbing that everyone wants to go further? When people nowadays – as is in fact variously announced – will not stop with love, where is it they are going? To worldly wisdom, petty calculation, to paltriness and misery, to all that can put man's divine origin in doubt? Would it not be better to remain standing at faith, and for the one who stands there to take care not to fall? For the movement of faith must be made continually on the strength of the absurd, though in such a way, be it noted, that one does not lose finitude but gains it all of a piece. I for my part can indeed describe the movements of faith, but I cannot perform them. When learning how to make swimming movements, one can hang in a belt from the ceiling; one may be said to describe the movements all right but one isn't swimming; likewise I can describe the movements of faith but when I am thrown into the water, although I may be said to be swimming (for I'm not among the waders), I make other movements, I make the movements of infinity, while faith does the opposite, having performed the movements of infinity it makes those of finitude. Lucky the one who can make those movements, he performs a marvel, and I shall never tire of admiring him. Whether it is Abraham or the servant in Abraham's house, whether a professor of philosophy or a poor serving-maid is for me absolutely immaterial, I look only at the movements. But those I do indeed look at and let myself be fooled neither by myself nor by anyone else. The knights of infinite resignation are readily recognizable, their gait is gliding, bold. But those who wear the jewel of faith can easily disappoint, for their exterior bears a remarkable similarity to what infinite resignation itself as much as faith scorns, namely the *bourgeois* philistine.

In my own experience I frankly admit to having found no reliable examples, though I would not deny on that ground that possibly every other person is one. Still, I have tried now in vain for several years to track one down. People commonly travel the world over to see rivers and mountains, new stars,

garish birds, freak fish, grotesque breeds of human; they fall
into an animal stupor that gapes at existence and they think
they have seen something. I am not concerned with this. But
if I knew where such a knight of faith lived I would journey
to him on foot, for this marvel concerns me absolutely. I would
not let him slip one instant, but watch every minute how he
makes the movements; I would consider myself maintained for
life and divide my time between looking at him and practising
the movements myself, thus devoting *all* my time to admiring
him. As I said, I haven't found such a one; still, I can very well
imagine him. Here he is. The acquaintance is struck, I am
introduced. The moment I first set eyes on him I thrust him
away, jump back, clasp my hands together and say half aloud:
'Good God! Is this the person, is it really him? He looks just
like a tax-gatherer.' Yet it is indeed him. I come a little closer,
watch the least movement in case some small, incongruous
optical telegraphic message from the infinite should appear, a
glance, expression, gesture, a sadness, a smile betraying the
infinite by its incongruity with the finite. No! I examine him
from top to toe, in case there should be some crack through
which the infinite peeped out. No! He is solid through and
through. His stance? Vigorous, it belongs altogether to finitude,
no smartly turned-out townsman taking a stroll out to Fresberg
on a Sunday afternoon treads the ground with surer foot; he
belongs altogether to the world, no *petit bourgeois* belongs to
it more. One detects nothing of the strangeness and superiority
that mark the knight of the infinite. This man takes pleasure,
takes part, in everything, and whenever one catches him
occupied with something his engagement has the persistence
of the worldly person whose soul is wrapped up in such things.
He minds his affairs. To see him at them you would think he
was some pen-pusher who had lost his soul to Italian book-
keeping, so attentive to detail is he. He takes a holiday on
Sundays. He goes to church. No heavenly glance or any other
sign of the incommensurable betrays him; if one didn't know
him it would be impossible to set him apart from the rest of
the crowd; for at most his hearty, lusty psalm-singing proves
that he has a good set of lungs. In the afternoon he takes a

walk in the woods. He delights in everything he sees, in the thronging humanity, the new omnibuses,[43] the Sound – to run across him on Strandveien you would think he was a shopkeeper having his fling, such is his way of taking pleasure; for he is not a poet and I have sought in vain to prise out of him the secret of any poetic incommensurability. Towards evening he goes home, his step tireless as a postman's. On the way it occurs to him that his wife will surely have some special little warm dish for his return, for example roast head of lamb with vegetables. If he were to meet a kindred spirit, he could continue as far as Østerport so as to converse with him about this dish with a passion befitting a *restaurateur*. As it happens he hasn't a penny and yet he firmly believes his wife has that delicacy waiting for him. If she has, to see him eat it would be a sight for superior people to envy and for plain folk to be inspired by, for his appetite is greater than Esau's. If his wife doesn't have the dish, curiously enough he is exactly the same. On the road he passes a building-site and meets another man. They talk together for a moment, he has a building raised in a jiffy, having all that's needed for that. The stranger leaves him thinking: 'That must have been a capitalist,' while my admirable knight thinks: 'Yes, if it came to that I could surely manage it.' He takes his ease at an open window and looks down on the square where he lives, at everything that goes on – a rat slipping under a board over the gutter, the children at play – with a composure befitting a sixteen-year-old girl. And yet he is no genius; I have tried in vain to spy out in him the incommensurability of the genius. He smokes his pipe in the evening: to see him you would swear it was the cheesemonger opposite vegetating in the dusk. Carefree as a devil-may-care good-for-nothing, he hasn't a worry in the world, and yet he purchases every moment that he lives, 'redeeming the seasonable time' at the dearest price;[44] not the least thing does he do except on the strength of the absurd. And yet, and yet – yes, it could drive me to fury, out of envy if for no other reason – and yet this man has made and is at every moment making the movement of infinity. He drains in infinite resignation the deep sorrow of existence, he knows the bliss of infinity, he has felt the pain of renouncing everything, whatever is most precious in the world, and yet to him finitude tastes just as good as to one who has never known anything higher, for his remaining in the finite bore no trace of a stunted, anxious training, and still he has this sense of being secure to take pleasure in it, as though it were the most certain thing of all. And yet, and yet the whole earthly form he presents is a new creation on the strength of the absurd. He resigned everything infinitely, and then took everything back on the strength of the absurd. He is continually making the movement of infinity, but he makes it with such accuracy and poise that he is continually getting finitude out of it, and not for a second would one suspect anything else. It is said that the dancer's hardest task is to leap straight into a definite position, so that not for a second does he have to catch at the position but stands there in it in the leap itself. Perhaps no dancer can do it – but that knight does it. The mass of humans live disheartened lives of earthly sorrow and joy, these are the sitters-out who will not join in the dance. The knights of infinity are dancers too and they have elevation. They make the upward movement and fall down again, and this too is no unhappy pastime, nor ungracious to behold. But when they come down they cannot assume the position straightaway, they waver an instant and the wavering shows they are nevertheless strangers in the world. This may be more or less evident, depending on their skill, but even the most skilled of these knights cannot hide the vacillation. One doesn't need to see them in the air, one only has to see them the moment they come and have come to earth to recognize them. But to be able to land in just that way, and in the same second to look as though one was up and walking, to transform the leap in life to a gait, to express the sublime in the pedestrian absolutely – that is something only the knight of faith can do – and it is the one and only marvel.

Yet this marvel can so easily deceive. I will therefore describe the movements in a particular case which can illustrate the respective relationships to reality, for it is these that everything turns on. A young lad falls in love with a princess, the content of his whole life lies in this love, and yet the relationship is one that cannot possibly be brought to fruition, be translated from ideality into reality.* The slaves of misery, the frogs in life's swamp, naturally exclaim: 'Such love is foolishness; the rich brewer's widow is just as good and sound a match.' Let them croak away undisturbed in the swamp. This is not the manner of the knight of infinite resignation, he does not renounce the love, not for all the glory in the world. He is no trifler. He first makes sure that this really is the content of his life, and his soul is too healthy and proud to squander the least thing on getting drunk. He is not cowardly, he is not afraid to let his love steal in upon his most secret, most hidden thoughts, to let it twine itself in countless coils around every ligament of his consciousness – if the love becomes unhappy he will never be able to wrench himself out of it. He feels a blissful rapture when he lets it tingle through every nerve, and yet his soul is as solemn as his who has emptied the cup of poison and feels the juice penetrate to every drop of blood – for this moment is life and death. Having thus imbibed all the love and absorbed himself in it, he does not lack the courage to attempt and risk everything. He reflects over his life's circumstances, he summons the swift thoughts that like trained doves obey his every signal, he waves his rod over them, and they rush off in all directions. But now when they all return as messengers of sorrow and explain to him that it is an impossibility, he becomes quiet, he dismisses them, he remains alone, and he performs the movement. If what I say here has any meaning the movement must take place properly.†

---

*Of course any other interest whatever in which an individual concentrates the whole of life's reality can, when it proves unrealizable, give rise to the movement of resignation. But I have chosen falling in love to illustrate the movements because this interest will no doubt be more readily understood and thus it relieves me of the need to make all the introductory comments which would be of direct interest to only a few.

† *This requires passion. Every movement of infinity occurs with passion, and no reflection can bring about a movement. That's the perpetual leap in life which explains the movement, while mediation is a chimera which in Hegel is supposed to explain everything and besides is the only thing he has never tried to explain.* Passion is needed even to make the familiar Socratic distinction between what one does and what one doesn't understand; naturally even more so in making the genuinely Socratic movement, that of ignorance. What we lack today is not reflection but passion. For that reason our age is really in a sense too tenacious of life to die, for dying is one of the most remarkable leaps, and a small verse has always greatly attracted me, because having wished himself all the good and simple things in life in five or six lines previously, the poet ends thus: *'ein seliger Sprung in die Ewigkeit'* [a blessed leap into eternity].

For the knight will then, in the first place, have the strength to concentrate the whole of his life's content and the meaning of reality in a single wish. If a person lacks this concentration, this focus, his soul is disintegrated from the start, and then he will never come to make the movement, he will act prudently in life like those capitalists who invest their capital in every kind of security so as to gain on the one what they lose on the other – in short, he is not a knight. Secondly, the knight will have the strength to concentrate the whole of the result of his reflection into one act of consciousness. If he lacks this focus his soul is disintegrated from the start and he will then never have time to make the movement, he will be forever running errands in life, never enter the eternal; for at the very moment he is almost there he will suddenly discover that he has forgotten something and so must go back. The next moment he will think it possible, and that is also quite correct; but through such considerations one never comes to make the movement; rather with their help one sinks ever deeper into the mire.

So the knight makes the movement, but what movement? Does he want to forget the whole thing? Because in that too there is a kind of concentration. No! for the knight does not contradict himself, and it is a contradiction to forget the whole of one's life's content and still be the same. He has no inclination to become another, seeing nothing at all great in that prospect. Only lower natures forget themselves and become something new. Thus the butterfly has altogether forgotten that it was a caterpillar, perhaps it can so completely forget in turn that it was a butterfly that it can become a fish. Deeper natures never forget themselves and never become something other than they were. So the knight will remember everything; but the memory is precisely the pain, and yet in his infinite resignation he is reconciled with existence. His love for the princess would take on for him the expression of an eternal love, would acquire a religious character, be transfigured into a love for the eternal being which, although it denied fulfilment, still reconciled him once more in the eternal consciousness of his love's validity in an eternal form that no reality can take from him. Fools and young people talk about everything being possible for a human

being. But that is a great mistake. Everything is possible
spiritually speaking, but in the finite world there is much that
is not possible. This impossibility the knight nevertheless makes
possible by his expressing it spiritually, but he expresses it
spiritually by renouncing it. The desire which would convey
him out into reality, but came to grief on an impossibility, now
bends inwards but is not lost thereby nor forgotten. At times
it is the unconscious workings of the desire in him which
awaken the memory, at others it is he himself that awakens
it, for he is too proud to want to let the whole content of his
life seem to have been but a fleeting affair of the moment. He
keeps this love young, and it grows with him in years and
beauty. On the other hand, he needs no finite occasion for its
growth. From the moment he made the movement the princess
is lost. He needs none of this erotic titillation of the nerves at
the sight of the loved one, etc., nor does he need in a finite
sense to be continually making his farewell, for his memory of
her is an eternal one, and he knows very well that those lovers
who are so eager to see one another one more time to say farewell are right to be eager, right to think it will be the last time;
for as soon as may be they will have forgotten one another.
He has grasped the deep secret that even in loving another one
should be sufficient unto oneself. He pays no further finite
attention to what the princess does, and just this proves that
he has made the movement infinitely. Here we have the
opportunity to see whether the movement in the individual is
proper or not. There was a person who also believed he had
made the movement, but time went by, the princess did something else, she married, say, a prince, and his soul lost the resilience of resignation.[45] He knew then that he had not made the
movement correctly; for one who has infinitely resigned is enough
unto himself. The knight does not cancel his resignation, he
keeps it, just as young as in the first instance, he never lets it
go, simply because he has made the movement infinitely. What
the princess does cannot disturb him, it is only lower natures
who have the law for their actions in someone else, the premisses
for their actions outside themselves. If, on the other hand, the
princess is similarly disposed there will be a beautiful develop-

ment. She will then introduce herself into that order of knighthood whose members are not admitted by ballot but which anyone can join who has the courage to admit him- or herself,
that order of knighthood which proves its immortality by
making no distinction between man and woman. She too will
keep her love young and sound, she too will have overcome
her agony, even though she does not, as the song says, 'lie by
her lord's side'.[46] These two will then be suited to each other
in all eternity, with such a strict-tempoed *harmonia praestabilita*
[pre-established harmony] that were some moment to come,
a moment with which they were nevertheless not concerned
finitely, for in the finite world they would grow old – were such
a moment to come which allowed their love its expression in
time, then they would be in a position to begin precisely where
they would have begun had they been united from the
beginning. The one, whether man or woman, who understands
this can never be deceived, for it is only lower natures who
imagine they are deceived. No girl who lacks this pride really
knows what it is to love, but if she is so proud, then all the
world's stratagems and ingenuity cannot deceive her.

In infinite resignation there is peace and repose; anyone who
wants it, who has not debased himself by – what is still worse
than being too proud – belittling himself, can discipline himself
into making this movement, which in its pain reconciles one
to existence. Infinite resignation is that shirt in the old fable.[47]
The thread is spun with tears, bleached by tears, the shirt sewn
in tears, but then it also gives better protection than iron and
steel. A defect of the fable is that a third party is able to make
the material. The secret in life is that everyone must sew it for
himself; and the remarkable thing is that a man can sew it just
as well as a woman. In infinite resignation there is peace and
repose and consolation in the pain, that is if the movement is
made properly. I could easily fill a whole book with the various
misunderstandings, awkward positions, and slovenly movements I have encountered in just my own slight experience.
People believe very little in spirit, yet it is precisely spirit that
is needed to make this movement; what matters is its not being
a one-sided result of *dira necessitas;*[48] the more it is that the more

doubtful it always is that the movement is proper. To insist that a frigid, sterile necessity is necessarily present is to say that no one may experience death before actually dying, which strikes me as crass materialism. Yet in our time people are less concerned with making pure movements. Suppose someone wanting to learn to dance said: 'For hundreds of years now one generation after another has been learning dance steps, it's high time I took advantage of this and began straight off with a set of quadrilles.' One would surely laugh a little at him; but in the world of spirit such an attitude is considered utterly plausible. What then is education? I had thought it was the curriculum the individual ran through in order to catch up with himself; and anyone who does not want to go through this curriculum will be little helped by being born into the most enlightened age.

Infinite resignation is the last stage before faith, so that anyone who has not made this movement does not have faith; for only in infinite resignation does my eternal validity become transparent to me, and only then can there be talk of grasping existence on the strength of faith.

Let us now have the knight of faith make his appearance in the case discussed. He does exactly the same as the other knight, he infinitely renounces the claim to the love which is the content of his life; he is reconciled in pain; but then comes the marvel, he makes one more movement, more wonderful than anything else, for he says: 'I nevertheless believe that I shall get her, namely on the strength of the absurd, on the strength of the fact that for God all things are possible.' The absurd is not one distinction among others embraced by understanding. It is not the same as the improbable, the unexpected, the unforeseen. The moment the knight resigned he was convinced of the impossibility, humanly speaking; that was a conclusion of the understanding, and he had energy enough to think it. In an infinite sense, however, it was possible, through renouncing it [as a finite possibility]; but then accepting that [possibility] is at the same time to have given it up, yet for the understanding there is no absurdity in possessing it, for it is only in the finite world that understanding rules and there it was and remains an impossibility. On this the knight of faith is just as clear: all that can save him is the absurd; and this he grasps by faith. Accordingly he admits the impossibility and at the same time believes the absurd; for were he to suppose that he had faith without recognizing the impossibility with all the passion of his soul and with all his heart, he would be deceiving himself, and his testimony would carry weight nowhere; since he would not even have come as far as infinite resignation.

Faith is therefore no aesthetic emotion, but something far higher, exactly because it presupposes resignation; it is not the immediate inclination of the heart but the paradox of existence. Thus that a young girl in the face of all difficulties rests assured that her desire will be fulfilled in no way means that her certainty is that of faith, even if she has been brought up by Christian parents and perhaps gone for a whole year to the pastor. She is convinced in all her childlike simplicity and innocence. This assurance too ennobles her nature and gives her a preternatural dimension, so that like a worker of wonders she can charm the finite powers of existence and make even stones weep, while on the other hand in her distraction she can just as well run to Herod as to Pilate and move the whole world with her pleas. Her conviction is ever so lovable, and one can learn much from her, but one thing one does not learn from her, how to make movements. Her certainty does not dare look the impossibility in the eye in the pain of resignation.

I can see then that it requires strength and energy and freedom of spirit to make the infinite movement of resignation; I can also see that it can be done. The next step dumbfounds me, my brain reels; for having made the movement of resignation, now on the strength of the absurd to get everything, to get one's desire, whole, in full, that requires more-than-human powers, it is a marvel. But at least I can see this, that the young girl's conviction is mere frivolity compared with a faith that is unshakeable even when it sees the impossibility. Whenever I want to make this movement I turn giddy, at the same moment I admire it absolutely and yet in that same instant an immense anxiety seizes my soul, for what is it to test God? And yet this is the movement of faith and remains that, however much philosophy, in order to confuse concepts, will have us suppose that it has faith, however much theology wants to sell it at a bargain price.

Resignation does not require faith, for what I win in resignation is my eternal consciousness, and that is a purely philosophical movement, which I venture upon when necessary, and which I can discipline myself into doing, for every time something finite out-distances me I starve myself until I make the movement; for my eternal consciousness is my love of God, and for me that is higher than anything. Resignation does not require faith, but it requires faith to get the slightest more than my eternal consciousness, for that [more] is the paradox. The movements are often confused. It is said that faith is needed in order to renounce everything; yes, even more strangely one hears people complain that they have lost faith and on consulting the scale to see where they are, we find curiously enough that they have come no further than the point where they should be making the infinite movement of resignation. Through resignation I renounce everything, this movement is one I do by myself, and when I do not do it that is because I am cowardly and weak and lack the enthusiasm and have no sense of the importance of the high dignity afforded to every human being, to be his own censor, a dignity greater by far than to be Censor General for the whole Roman Republic. This movement is one that I make by myself, so what I win is myself in my eternal consciousness, in a blessed compliance with my love for the eternal being. Through faith I don't renounce anything, on the contrary in faith I receive everything, exactly in the way it is said that one whose faith is like a mustard seed can move mountains.[49] It takes a purely human courage to renounce the whole of temporality in order to win eternity, but I do indeed win it and cannot in all eternity renounce that, for that would be a self-contradiction; but it takes a paradoxical and humble courage then to grasp the whole of temporality on the strength of the absurd, and that courage is the courage of faith. Through faith Abraham did not renounce his claim on Isaac, through his faith he received Isaac. That rich young man, by virtue of his resignation, should have given everything away, but once he had done so the knight of faith would have to say to him: 'On the strength of the absurd you shall get every penny back, believe that!' And these words should by no means be a matter of indifference to the once rich young man; for if he gave his possessions away because he was bored with them, then his resignation was in a sorry state.

Temporality, finitude is what it all turns on. I am able by my own strength to renounce everything, and then find peace and repose in the pain; I can put up with everything even if that demon, more horrifying than the skull and bones that put terror into men's hearts – even if madness itself were to hold up the fool's costume before my eyes and I could tell from its look that it was I who was to put it on; I can still save my soul so long as it is more important for me that my love of God should triumph in me than my worldly happiness. A man can still, in that last moment, concentrate his whole soul in a single glance towards the heaven from which all good gifts come, and this glance is something both he and the one he seeks understand; it means he has nevertheless remained true to his love. Then he will calmly put on the costume. He who lacks this romanticism has sold his soul, whether he received a kingdom for it or a paltry piece of silver. But by my own strength I cannot get the least little thing of what belongs to finitude; for I am continually using my energy to renounce everything. By my own strength I can give up the princess, and I shall be no sulker but find joy and peace and repose in my pain, but with my own strength I cannot get her back again, for all that strength is precisely what I use to renounce my claim on her. But by faith, says that marvellous knight, by faith you will get her on the strength of the absurd.[50]

Alas, this movement is one I cannot make! As soon as I want to begin it everything turns around and I flee back to the pain of resignation. I can swim in life, but for this mysterious floating I am too heavy. To exist in such a way that my opposition to existence expresses itself every instant as the most beautiful and safest harmony, that I cannot. And yet it must be glorious to get the princess, I say so every instant and the knight of resignation who doesn't say it is a deceiver, he has not had just one desire and he has not kept his desire young in its pain. Some might find it convenient enough that the desire is no longer alive, that the smart of pain has dulled; but such people are no knights. A free-born soul who caught himself at this would despise himself and make a fresh start, and above all not allow himself to be deceived in his soul. And yet it must be wonderful to get the princess, and yet it is only the knight of faith who is happy, only he is heir apparent to the finite, whereas the knight of resignation is a stranger, a foreigner. To get the princess in this way, to live in joy and happiness, in her company day in and day out – we have to allow, of course, that the knight of resignation, too, may get the princess, even though he has clearly perceived the impossibility of their future happiness – thus to live joyfully and happily in this way every moment on the strength of the absurd, every moment to see the sword hanging over the loved one's head and yet find, not repose in the pain of resignation, but joy on the strength of the absurd – that is wonderful. The one who does that, he is great, the only great one, the thought of it stirs my soul, which was never sparing in its admiration of greatness.

Now if everyone in my generation unwilling to stop at faith is really someone who has understood life's horror, has grasped Daub's[31] meaning when he says that a soldier standing guard alone with a loaded gun by a powder magazine on a stormy night gets strange thoughts; if all those unwilling to stop at faith really are people who possess the strength of soul to grasp, and give themselves time to be alone with, the thought that what they wished was impossible; if all who are unwilling to stop at faith have really reconciled themselves in pain and been reconciled by pain; if all those unwilling to stop at faith have in addition (and unless they have done all this other they need not trouble themselves in matters of faith) performed that marvel, grasped the whole of existence on the strength of the absurd – then what I am writing is a speech in the highest praise of my generation by the least in it, by the one who could only make the movement of resignation. But why will they not *stop* at faith, why do we sometimes hear of people blushing to admit they have faith? That I cannot grasp. Should I ever come so far as to manage this movement, I'd drive thereafter with a coach-and-four.

Is it really the case, can all the *bourgeois* philistinism I see in life, and which I allow only my deeds and not my words to condemn, really be not what it seems? Is it really this marvel? That is certainly conceivable, for our hero of faith did indeed bear a striking resemblance to it, for our hero of faith was not even an ironist and humorist but something still higher. A lot is said in our time about irony and humour, particularly by people who have never succeeded in practising them but who nevertheless know how to explain everything. I am not altogether unfamiliar with these two passions, I know a little more about them than is to be found in German and German-Danish compendia. Therefore I know that these two passions differ essentially from the passion of faith. Irony and humour reflect also upon themselves and so belong in the sphere of infinite resignation, they owe their resilience to the individual's incommensurability with reality.[52]

The last movement, the paradoxical movement of faith I cannot perform, be it a duty or whatever – though in fact I would be most willing to do it. Whether anyone has the right to say this must be up to him; it is a matter between him and the eternal being who is the object of faith whether he can reach an amicable agreement in this respect. What everyone can do, on the other hand, is perform the infinite movement of resignation, and I for my part would not think twice about pronouncing anyone a coward who thinks he can't. With faith it is another matter. But what no one has the right to do is let others suppose that faith is something inferior or that it is an easy matter, when in fact it is the greatest and most difficult of all.

Some understand the story of Abraham in another way. They praise God's mercy for giving him Isaac once again, the whole thing was just a trial. A trial – that can say a lot or little, yet the whole thing is as quickly done with as said. One mounts a winged horse, that very instant one is on the mountain in Moriah, the same instant one sees the ram. One forgets that Abraham rode on an ass, which can keep up no more than a leisurely pace, that he had a three-day journey, that he needed time to chop the firewood, bind Isaac, and sharpen the knife.

And yet one praises Abraham! The speaker might just as well sleep until fifteen minutes before speaking, his hearer might just as well sleep throughout the speech, since it all goes so smoothly, without trouble from either side. Should someone present be suffering from insomnia, that person might go home, sit down in a corner, and think: 'It's all over in a second, if you'll just wait a minute you'll see the ram and the trial is over.' Were the speaker to meet him in that state then I imagine he would advance on him in all his dignity and say: 'Wretch, that you can let your soul sink into such folly; there is no miracle, and all life is a trial.' The more effusive the speaker became the more heated he would grow and the better pleased with himself, and while he had noticed no congestion of the blood when speaking about Abraham, he could now feel the vein swelling on his forehead. He might perhaps be struck dumb were the sinner, calmly and with dignity, to reply: 'But that's what you preached last Sunday.'

So let us either forget all about Abraham or learn how to be horrified at the monstrous paradox which is the significance of his life, so that we can understand that our time like any other can be glad if it has faith. If Abraham is not a nonentity, a ghost, a piece of pomp one uses to pass time away, the mistake can never lie in the sinner's wanting to do like him; rather it is a question of seeing the greatness of Abraham's deed, so that the person may judge for himself whether he has the inclination and courage to be tried in such a thing. The comic contradiction in the speaker's behaviour was that he made Abraham into something insignificant and yet would forbid the other from carrying on in the same manner.

Should one perhaps not dare to speak about Abraham? I think one should. If I myself were to talk about him I would first depict the pain of the trial. For that I would suck all the fear, distress, and torment out of the father's suffering, like a leech, in order to be able to describe all that Abraham suffered while still believing. I would remind people that the journey lasted three days and well into the fourth; yes, those three-and-a-half days should be infinitely longer than the two thousand years separating me from Abraham. Then I would remind them that everyone, as I believe, should feel able to change their mind before beginning on such a thing, that it is possible at every moment to retract and turn back. If one does this I see no danger; nor am I afraid of arousing a desire in people to be put to the test like Abraham. But if one wants to market a cut-price version of Abraham and then still admonish people not to do what Abraham did, then that's just laughable.

What I intend now is to extract from the story of Abraham its dialectical element, in the form of *problemata*, in order to see how monstrous a paradox faith is, a paradox capable of making a murder into a holy act well pleasing to God, a paradox which gives Isaac back to Abraham, which no thought can grasp because faith begins precisely where thinking leaves off.

PROBLEMA I

Is there a teleological suspension of the ethical?

The ethical as such is the universal, and as the universal it applies to everyone, which can be put from another point of view by saying that it applies at every moment. It rests immanently in itself, has nothing outside itself that is its *telos* [end, purpose] but is itself the *telos* for everything outside, and when that is taken up into it, it has no further to go. Seen as an immediate, no more than sensate and psychic, being, the single individual is the particular that has its *telos* in the universal, and the individual's ethical task is always to express himself in this, to abrogate his particularity so as to become the universal. As soon as the single individual wants to assert himself in his particularity, in direct opposition to the universal, he sins, and only by recognizing this can he again reconcile himself with the universal. Whenever, having entered the universal, the single individual feels an urge to assert his particularity, he is in a state of temptation,[53] from which he can extricate himself only by surrendering his particularity to the universal in repentance. If that is the highest that can be said of man and his existence, then the ethical and a person's eternal blessedness, which is his *telos* in all eternity and at every moment, are identical; for in that case it would be a contradiction to say that one surrendered that *telos* (i.e. suspended it *teleologically*) since by suspending the *telos* one would be forfeiting it, while what is said to be suspended in this sense is not forfeited but preserved in something higher, the latter being precisely its *telos*.

If that is the case, then Hegel is right in his 'Good and Conscience' where he discusses man seen merely as the single individual and regards this way of seeing him as a 'moral form of evil' to be annulled in the teleology of the ethical life,[54] so that the individual who stays at this stage is either in sin or in a state of temptation. Where Hegel goes wrong, on the other hand, is in talking about faith,[55] in not protesting loudly and clearly against the honour and glory enjoyed by Abraham as the father of faith when he should really be remitted to some lower court for trial and exposed as a murderer.[56]

For faith is just this paradox, that the single individual is higher than the universal, though in such a way, be it noted, that the movement is repeated, that is, that, having been in the universal, the single individual now sets himself apart as the particular above the universal. If that is not faith, then Abraham is done for and faith has never existed in the world, just because it has always existed. For if the ethical life is the highest and nothing incommensurable is left over in man, except in the sense of what is evil, i.e. the single individual who is to be expressed in the universal, then one needs no other categories than those of the Greek philosophers, or whatever can be logically deduced from them. This is something Hegel, who has after all made some study of the Greeks, ought not to have kept quiet about.

One not infrequently hears people who prefer to lose themselves in clichés rather than studies say that light shines over the Christian world, while paganism is shrouded in darkness. This kind of talk has always struck me as strange, since any reasonably deep thinker, any reasonably serious artist will still seek rejuvenation in the eternal youth of the Greeks. The explanation may be that they know not what to say, only that they have to say something. There is nothing wrong with saying that paganism did not have faith, but if this is to mean anything one must be a little clearer what one means by faith, otherwise one falls back into those clichés. It is easy to explain the whole of existence, faith included, and he is not the worst reckoner in life who counts on being admired for having such an explanation; for it is as Boileau says: *'un sot trouve toujours un plus sot, qui l'admire'* ['a fool can always find a greater fool who admires him'].[57]

Faith is just this paradox, that the single individual as the particular is higher than the universal, is justified before the latter, not as subordinate but superior, though in such a way, be it noted, that it is the single individual who, having been subordinate to the universal as the particular, now by means of the universal becomes that individual who, as the particular, stands in an absolute relation to the absolute. This position cannot be mediated, for all mediation occurs precisely by virtue of the universal;[58] it is and remains in all eternity a paradox, inaccessible to thought. And yet faith *is* this paradox. Or else (these are implications which I would ask the reader always to bear in mind, though it would be too complicated for me to spell them out each time) – or else faith has never existed just because it has always existed. And Abraham is done for.

That the individual can easily take this paradox for a temptation is true enough. But one should not keep it quiet on that account. True enough, too, that many people may have a natural aversion to the paradox, but that is no reason for making faith into something else so that they too can have it; while those who do have faith should be prepared to offer some criterion for distinguishing the paradox from a temptation.

Now the story of Abraham contains just such a teleological suspension of the ethical. There has been no want of sharp intellects and sound scholars who have found analogies to it. Their wisdom amounts to the splendid principle that basically everything is the same. If one looks a little closer I doubt very much whether one will find in the whole world a single analogy, except a later one that proves nothing, for the fact remains that Abraham represents faith, and that faith finds its proper expression in him whose life is not only the most paradoxical conceivable, but so paradoxical that it simply cannot be thought. He acts on the strength of the absurd; for it is precisely the absurd that as the single individual he is higher than the universal. This paradox cannot be mediated; for as soon as he tries Abraham will have to admit that he is in a state of temptation, and in that case he will never sacrifice Isaac, or if he has done so he must return repentantly to the universal. On the strength of the absurd he got Isaac back. Abraham is therefore at no instant the tragic hero, but something quite different, either a murderer or a man of faith. The middle-term that saves the tragic hero is something Abraham lacks. That is why I can understand a tragic hero, but not Abraham, even though in a certain lunatic sense I admire him more than all others.

Abraham's relation to Isaac, ethically speaking, is quite simply this, that the father should love the son more than himself. Yet within its own compass the ethical has several rankings; let us see whether this story contains any such higher expression of the ethical which might explain his behaviour ethically, justify him ethically for suspending the ethical duty to the son, yet without thereby exceeding the ethical's own teleology.

When an enterprise involving a whole nation is prevented, when such an enterprise is brought to a halt by heaven's disfavour, when divine wrath sends a dead calm which mocks every effort, when the soothsayer performs his sad task and proclaims that the deity demands a young girl as a sacrifice – then it is with heroism that the father has to make that sacrifice. Nobly will he hide his grief though he could wish he were 'the lowly man who dares to weep'[59] and not the king who must bear himself as befits a king. And however solitarily the pain enters his breast, for he has only three confidants among his people,[60] soon the entire population will be privy to his pain, but also to his deed, to the fact that for the well-being of the whole he was willing to offer that girl, his daughter, this lovely young maiden. Oh, what bosom! What fair cheeks! What flaxen hair![61] And the daughter will touch him with her tears, and the father avert his face, but the hero will raise the knife. And when the news of this reaches the ancestral home all the beauteous maidens of Greece will blush with animation, and were the daughter a bride the betrothed would not be angered but proud to have been party to the father's deed, because the maiden belonged to him more tenderly than to the father.

When that bold judge, who saved Israel in the hour of need binds God and himself in one breath with the same promise, then it is with heroism that he is to transform the young girl's jubilation, the beloved daughter's joy, to sorrow, and all Israel will grieve with her maidenly youth; but every free-born man will understand Jephthah,[62] every stout-hearted woman admire him, and every maiden in Israel will want to do as his daughter; for what good would it be for Jephthah to triumph by making his promise but fail to keep it? Would the victory not be taken once more from the people?

When a son forgets his duty, when the State entrusts the father with the sword of judgement, when the laws demand punishment at the father's hand, then it is with heroism that the father must forget that the guilty one is his son. Nobly will he hide his pain, but in the nation there will be not one, not even the son, who fails to admire the father, and every time the laws of Rome are interpreted it will be recalled that many interpreted them more learnedly but none more gloriously than Brutus.[63]

On the other hand, if it had been while his fleet was being borne by wind under full sail to its destination that Agamemnon had sent that messenger who brought Iphigenia to the sacrifice; if unbound by any promise that would decide the fate of his people Jephthah had said to his daughter: 'Sorrow now for two months henceforth over the short day of your youth, for I shall sacrifice you'; if Brutus had had a righteous son and still called upon the lictors to execute him – who would understand them? If to the question, why did you do it?, these three had replied: 'It is a trial in which we are being tested', would one then have understood them better?

When at the decisive moment Agamemnon, Jephthah, and Brutus heroically overcome their pain, have heroically given up the loved one, and have only the outward deed to perform, then never a noble soul in the world will there be but sheds tears of sympathy for their pain, tears of admiration for their deed. But if at that decisive moment these three men had added to the heroism with which they bore their pain the little words 'It won't happen', who then would understand them? If in explanation they added: 'We believe it on the strength of the absurd', who then would understand them better? For who would not readily understand that it was absurd? But who would understand that for that reason one could believe it?

The difference between the tragic hero and Abraham is obvious enough. The tragic hero stays within the ethical. He lets an expression of the ethical have its *telos* in a higher expression of the ethical; he reduces the ethical relation between father and son, or daughter and father, to a sentiment that has its dialectic in its relation to the idea of the ethical life. Here, then, there can be no question of a teleological suspension of the ethical itself.

With Abraham it is different. In his action he overstepped the ethical altogether, and had a higher *telos* outside it, in relation to which he suspended it. For how could one ever bring Abraham's action into relationship with the universal? How could any point of contact ever be discovered between what Abraham did and the universal other than that Abraham overstepped it? It is not to save a nation, not to uphold the idea of the State, that Abraham did it, not to appease angry gods. If there was any question of the deity's being angry, it could only have been Abraham he was angry with, and Abraham's whole action stands in no relation to the universal, it is a purely private undertaking. While, then, the tragic hero is great through his deed's being an expression of the ethical life,[64] Abraham is great through an act of purely personal virtue. There is no higher expression of the ethical in Abraham's life than that the father shall love the son. The ethical in the sense of the ethical life is quite out of the question. In so far as the universal was there at all it was latent in Isaac, concealed as it were in his loins,[65] and it would have to cry out with Isaac's mouth: 'Don't do it, you are destroying everything.'

Then why does Abraham do it? For God's sake, and what is exactly the same, for his own. He does it for the sake of God because God demands this proof of his faith; he does it for his own sake in order to be able to produce the proof. The unity here is quite properly expressed in the saying in which this relationship has always been described: it is a trial, a temptation. A temptation, but what does that mean? What we usually call a temptation is something that keeps a person from carrying out a duty, but here the temptation is the ethical itself which would keep him from doing God's will. But then what is the duty? For the duty is precisely the expression of God's will.

Here we see the need for a new category for understanding Abraham.[66] Such a relationship to the divine is unknown to paganism. The tragic hero enters into no private relationship with God, but the ethical is the divine and therefore the paradox in the divine can be mediated in the universal.

Abraham cannot be mediated, which can also be put by saying he cannot speak. The moment I speak I express the universal, and when I do not no one can understand me. So the moment Abraham wants to express himself in the universal, he has to say that his situation is one of temptation, for he has no higher expression of the universal that overrides the universal he transgresses.

Thus while Abraham arouses my admiration, he also appals me. The person who denies himself and sacrifices himself for duty gives up the finite in order to grasp on to the infinite; he is secure enough. The tragic hero gives up what is certain for what is still more certain, and the eye of the beholder rests confidently upon him. But the person who gives up the universal to grasp something still higher that is not the universal, what does he do? Can this be anything but temptation? And if it were something else but the individual were mistaken, what salvation is there for him? He suffers all the pain of the tragic hero, he brings all his joy in the world to nothing, he abandons everything, and perhaps the same instant debars himself from that exalted joy so precious to him that he would buy it at any price. That person the beholder cannot at all understand, nor let his eye rest upon him with confidence. Perhaps what the believer intends just cannot be done, after all it is unthinkable. Or if it could be done and the individual had misunderstood the deity, what salvation would there be for him? The tragic hero, he needs tears and he claims them; yes, where was that envious eye so barren as not to weep with Agamemnon, but where was he whose soul was so confused as to presume to weep for Abraham? The tragic hero has done with his deed at a definite moment in time, but in the course of time he achieves something no less important, he seeks out the one whose soul is beset with sorrow, whose breast cannot draw air for its stifled sighs, whose thoughts, weighed down with tears, hang heavy upon him; he appears before him, he breaks the spell of grief, loosens the corset, coaxes forth the tear by making the sufferer forget his own suffering in his. Abraham one cannot weep over. One

approaches him with a *horror religiosus* [holy terror] like that
in which Israel approached Mount Sinai. What if the lonely man
who climbs the mountain in Moriah, whose peak soars heaven-
high over the plains of Aulis, is not a sleepwalker who treads
surefootedly over the abyss, while someone standing at the foot
of the mountain, seeing him there, trembles with anxiety and
out of respect and fear dares not even shout to him – what if he
should be distracted, what if he has made a mistake? – Thanks!
And thanks again, to whoever holds out to one who has been
assaulted and left naked by life's sorrows, holds out to him the
leaf of the word with which to hide his misery. Thanks to you,
great Shakespeare!, you who can say everything, everything,
everything exactly as it is – and yet why was this torment one
you never gave voice to? Was it perhaps that you kept it to
yourself, like the beloved whose name one still cannot bear the
world to mention?[67] For a poet buys this power of words to utter
all the grim secrets of others at the cost of a little secret he himself
cannot utter, and a poet is not an apostle, he casts devils out only
by the power of the devil.[68]

But now when the ethical is thus teleologically suspended,
how does the single individual in whom it is suspended exist?
He exists as the particular in opposition to the universal. Does
this mean he sins? For this is the form of sin looked at ideally,
just as the fact that the child does not sin because it is not
conscious of its own existence as such does not mean that,
looked at ideally, its existence is not that of sin or that the ethical
does not make its demands of the child at every moment. If
this form cannot be said to repeat itself in a way other than
that of sin, then judgement has been delivered upon Abraham.
Then how did Abraham exist? He had faith. That is the paradox
that keeps him at the extremity and which he cannot make
clear to anyone else, for the paradox is that he puts himself
as the single individual in an absolute relation to the absolute.
Is he justified? His justification is, once again, the paradox; for
if he is the paradox it is not by virtue of being anything universal,
but of being the particular.

How does the single individual assure himself that he is
justified? It is a simple enough matter to level the whole of

existence down to the idea of the State or to a concept of society.[69] If one does that one can no doubt also mediate; for in this way one does not come to the paradox at all, to the single individual's as such being higher than the universal, which I can also put pointedly in a proposition of Pythagoras's, that the odd numbers are more perfect than the even. Should one happen to catch word of an answer in the direction of the paradox in our time, it will no doubt go like this: 'That's to be judged by the outcome.' A hero who has become the scandal of his generation,[70] aware that he is a paradox that cannot be understood, cries undaunted to his contemporaries: 'The future will show I was right!' This cry is heard less frequently nowadays, for as our age to its detriment produces no heroes, so it has the advantage that it also produces few caricatures. Whenever nowadays we hear the words 'That's to be judged by the outcome' we know immediately with whom we have the honour of conversing. Those who speak thus are a populous tribe which, to give them a common name, I shall call the 'lecturers'. They live in their thoughts, secure in life, they have a *permanent* position and *sure* prospects in a well-organized State; they are separated by centuries, even millennia, from the convulsions of existence; they have no fear that such things could happen again; what would the police and the newspapers say? Their lifework is to judge the great, to judge them according to the outcome. Such conduct in respect of greatness betrays a strange mixture of arrogance and pitifulness, arrogance because they feel called to pass judgement, pitifulness because they feel their lives unrelated in even the remotest manner to those of the great. Surely anyone with a speck of *erectior ingenii* [nobility of mind] cannot become so completely the cold and clammy mollusc as to lose sight altogether, in approaching the great, of the fact that ever since the Creation it has been accepted practice for the outcome to come last, and that if one is really to learn something from the great it is precisely the beginning one must attend to. If anyone on the verge of action should judge himself according to the outcome, he would never begin. Even though the result may gladden the whole world, that cannot help the hero; for he knows the result only when the whole thing is over, and that is not how he becomes a hero, but by virtue of the fact that he began.

But in any case the outcome in its dialectic (in so far as it is finitude's answer to the infinite question) is totally incompatible with the existence of the hero. Or are we to take it that Abraham was justified in relating himself as the single individual to the universal by the fact that he got Isaac by a *marvel*? Had Abraham actually sacrificed Isaac, would that have meant he was less justified?

But it is the outcome that arouses our curiosity, as with the conclusion of a book; one wants nothing of the fear, the distress, the paradox. One flirts with the outcome aesthetically; it comes as unexpectedly and yet as effortlessly as a prize in the lottery; and having heard the outcome one is improved. And yet no robber of temples hard-labouring in chains is so base a criminal as he who plunders the holy in this way, and not even Judas, who sold his master for thirty pieces of silver, is more contemptible than the person who would thus offer greatness for sale.

It goes against my nature to speak inhumanly of greatness, to let its grandeur fade into an indistinct outline at an immense distance, or represent it as great without the human element in it coming to the fore – whence it ceases to be the great; for it is not what happens to me that makes me great, but what I do, and there is surely no one who thinks that anyone became great by winning the big lottery prize. Even of a person born in humble circumstances I ask that he should not be so inhuman towards himself as to be unable to think of the king's castle except at a distance and by dreaming of its grandeur indistinctly, wanting to exalt it and simultaneously destroying its grandeur by exalting it in such a debasing way. I ask that he be human enough to approach and bear himself with confidence and dignity there too. He should not be so inhuman as shamelessly to want to violate every rule of respect by storming into the king's salon straight from the street – he loses more by doing that than the king; on the contrary he should find pleasure in observing every rule of decorum with a glad and confident enthusiasm, which is just what will make him frank and open-hearted. This is only an analogy, for the difference here is only a very imperfect expression of the spiritual distance. I ask everyone not to think so inhumanly of himself as to dare not set foot in those palaces where not just the memory of the chosen lives on but the chosen themselves. He should not push himself shamelessly forward and thrust upon them his kinship with them, he should feel happy every time he bows before them, but be frank and confident and always something more than a cleaning woman; for unless he wants to be more than that he will never come in there. And what will help him are exactly the fear and distress in which the great are tried, for otherwise, at least if there is a drop of red blood in him, they will merely arouse his righteous envy. And whatever can only be great at a distance, whatever people want to exalt with empty and hollow phrases, that they themselves reduce to nothing.

Was there ever in the world anyone as great as that blessed woman, the mother of God, the Virgin Mary? And yet how do people speak of her? To say she was favoured among women doesn't make her great, and if it were not for the odd fact that those who listen can think as inhumanly as those who speak, surely every young girl would ask, why am I not favoured too? And had I nothing more to say I should by no means dismiss such a question as stupid; for as regards favours, abstractly considered, everyone is equally entitled. What is left out is the distress, the fear, the paradox. My thought is as pure as the next man's and surely the thought of anyone able to think in this way will be pure; if not, something dreadful is in store; for a person who has once called these images to mind cannot be rid of them again, and if he sins against them, then in their quiet wrath, more terrifying than the clamour of ten voracious critics, they will wreak their awful vengeance on him. No doubt Mary bore the child miraculously, but it went with Mary 'after the manner of women',[71] and such a time is one of fear, distress, and paradox. No doubt the angel was a ministering spirit, but he was not an obliging one who went round to all the other young girls in Israel and said: 'Do not despise Mary, something out of the ordinary is happening to her.' The angel came only to Mary, and no one could understand her. Yet what woman

was done greater indignity than Mary, and isn't it true here
too that those whom God blesses he damns in the same breath?
This is the spirit's understanding of Mary, and she is not at all
– as it offends me to say, though even more so that people have
mindlessly and irresponsibly thought of her thus – she is not
at all the fine lady sitting in her finery and playing with a divine
child. Yet for saying notwithstanding, 'Behold the handmaid
of the Lord',[72] she is great, and it seems to me that it should
not be difficult to explain why she became the mother of God.
She needs no worldly admiration, as little as Abraham needs
our tears, for she was no heroine and he no hero, but both
of them became greater than that, not by any means by being
relieved of the distress, the agony, and the paradox, but because
of these.

Great indeed it is when the poet presents his tragic hero for
popular admiration and dares to say: 'Weep for him, for he
deserves it'; for there is greatness in meriting the tears of those
who deserve to shed them; great indeed for the poet to dare
hold the crowd in check, dare discipline people into testing their
own worthiness to weep for the hero, for the waste-water of
snivellers is a degradation of the holy. But greater than all these
is that the knight of faith dares to say even to the noble person
who would weep for him: 'Do not weep for me, but weep for
yourself.'

One is stirred, one harks back to those beautiful times, sweet
tender longings lead one to the goal of one's desire, to see Christ
walking about in the promised land. One forgets the fear, the
distress, the paradox. Was it so easy a matter not to be mistaken?
Was it not a fearful thought that this man who walked among
the others was God? Was it not terrifying to sit down to eat
with him? Was it so easy a matter to become an apostle? But
the outcome, eighteen centuries, that helps; it helps that
shabby deception wherein one deceives oneself and others. I do
not feel brave enough to wish to be contemporary with such
events, but for that reason I do not judge harshly of those
who were mistaken, nor think meanly of those who saw the
truth.

But now I return to Abraham. In the time before the outcome

either Abraham was a murderer every minute or we stay with the paradox which is higher than all mediation.

So Abraham's story contains a teleological suspension of the ethical. He has, as the single individual, become higher than the universal. This is the paradox which cannot be mediated. How he got into it is just as inexplicable as how he stayed in it. If this is not how it is with Abraham, then he is not even a tragic hero but a murderer. To want to go on calling him the father of faith, to talk of this to those who are only concerned with words, is thoughtless. A tragic hero can become a human being by his own strength, but not the knight of faith. When a person sets out on the tragic hero's admittedly hard path there are many who could lend him advice; but he who walks the narrow path of faith no one can advise, no one understand. Faith is a marvel, and yet no human being is excluded from it; for that in which all human life is united is passion,* and faith is a passion.

---

*Lessing has somewhere made similar remarks from a purely aesthetic point of view. In the passage in question he actually wants to show that sorrow too can express itself with wit. To that end he quotes the words spoken on a particular occasion by the unfortunate English king, Edward II. As contrast he quotes from Diderot: a story of a farmer's wife and a remark of hers, and then continues: 'That too was wit, and the wit of a peasant at that; but the situation made it inevitable. Consequently one mustn't try to find the excuse for the witty expression of pain and of sorrow in the fact that the person who uttered them was superior, well-educated, intelligent, and witty as well, *for the passions make all men again equal* ... the explanation lies in the fact that in the same situation probably everyone would have said the same thing. The peasant woman's thought is one a queen might just as well have had, just as what the king said on that occasion could, and no doubt would, have been said by a peasant.'[3]

PROBLEMA II

Is there an absolute duty to God?

The ethical is the universal and as such, in turn, the divine. It is therefore correct to say that all duty is ultimately duty to God; but if one cannot say more one says in effect that really I have no duty to God. The duty becomes duty to God by being referred to God, but I do not enter into relation with God in the duty itself. Thus it is a duty to love one's neighbour; it is a duty in so far as it is referred to God; yet it is not God that I come in relation to in the duty but the neighbour I love. If, in this connection, I then say that it is my duty to love God, I in fact only utter a tautology, in so far as 'God' is understood in an altogether abstract sense as the divine: i.e. the universal, i.e. duty. The whole of human existence is in that case entirely self-enclosed, as a sphere, and the ethical is at once the limit and completion. God becomes an invisible, vanishing point, an impotent thought, and his power is to be found only in the ethical, which fills all existence. So if it should occur to someone to want to love God in some other sense than that mentioned, he is merely being extravagant and loves a phantom which, if it only had the strength to speak, would say to him: 'Stay where you belong, I don't ask for your love.' If it should occur to someone to want to love God in another way, this love would be suspect, like the love referred to by Rousseau when he talks of a person's loving the Kaffirs instead of his neighbour.

Now if all this is correct, if there is nothing incommensurable in a human life, but any incommensurability were due only to some chance from which nothing followed so far as existence is looked at in light of the Idea, then Hegel would be right. But where he is wrong is in talking about faith or in letting Abraham be looked on as its father; for in this latter he has passed sentence both on Abraham and on faith. In the Hegelian philosophy *das Äussere* (*die Entäusserung*) [the outer, the externalization] is higher than *das Innere* [the inner]. This is often illustrated by an example. The child is *das Innere*, the man *das Äussere*; which is why the child is determined precisely by the outer, and conversely the man as *das Äussere* by the inner.[74] Faith, on the contrary, is this paradox, that interiority is higher than exteriority, or to recall again an expression we used above, that the odd number is higher than the even.

In the ethical view of life, then, it is the individual's task to divest himself of the determinant of interiority and give it an expression in the exterior. Whenever the individual shrinks from doing so, whenever he wants to stay inside, or slip back into, the inner determinant of feeling, mood, etc., he commits an offence, he is in a state of temptation. The paradox of faith is this, that there is an interiority that is incommensurable with the exterior, an interiority which, it should be stressed, is not identical with the first [that of the child], but is a new interiority. This must not be overlooked. Recent philosophy has allowed itself without further ado to substitute the immediate for 'faith'.[75] If one does that it is ridiculous to deny that faith has existed through all ages. Faith in such a case keeps fairly ordinary company, it belongs with feeling, mood, idiosyncrasy, hysteria and the rest. So far philosophy is right to say one should not stop at that. But there is nothing to warrant philosophy's speaking in this manner. Prior to faith there is a movement of infinity, and only then enters faith, *nec opinate* [unexpectedly], on the strength of the absurd. This I am very well able to understand, without claiming thereby to have faith. If faith is no more than what philosophy passes it off as then Socrates himself already went further, much further, rather than the converse, that he didn't come that far. He made the movement of infinity intellectually. His ignorance is the infinite resignation. That task is in itself a match for human strength, even if people nowadays scorn it; yet it is only when this has been done, only when the individual has exhausted himself in the infinite, that he reaches the point where faith can emerge.

Then faith's paradox is this, that the single individual is higher than the universal, that the single individual (to recall a theological distinction less in vogue these days) determines his relation to the universal through his relation to the absolute, not his relation to the absolute through his relation to the universal. The paradox can also be put by saying that there is an absolute duty to God; for in this tie of obligation the individual relates himself absolutely, as the single individual, to the absolute. When people now say that it is a duty to love God, it is in a sense quite different from the above; for if this duty is absolute the ethical is reduced to the relative. It doesn't follow, nevertheless, that [the ethical] is to be done away with. Only that it gets a quite different expression, the paradoxical expression, so that, e.g., love of God can cause the knight of faith to give his love of his neighbour the opposite expression to that which is his duty ethically speaking.

Unless this is how it is, faith has no place in existence; and faith is then a temptation, and Abraham is done for, since he gave in to it.

This paradox does not allow of mediation; for it rests precisely on the single individual's being only the single individual. As soon as this individual wants to express his absolute duty in the universal, becomes conscious of it in the latter, he knows he is in a state of temptation, and then, even if he otherwise resists the temptation, he does not come to fulfil that so-called absolute duty, and if he does not resist it he sins even if *realiter* [independently of his inclination, wishes, state of mind] his act is the one that was his absolute duty. Thus what could Abraham have done? If he had wanted to say to someone: 'I love Isaac more than everything in the world, and that's why it is so hard for me to sacrifice him', the person would surely have shaken his head and said: 'Then why sacrifice him?', or if he was a perceptive fellow perhaps he might even have seen through Abraham, realized that he was betraying feelings which stood in flagrant contradiction with his deed.

In the story of Abraham we find just such a paradox. Ethically speaking his relation to Isaac is this, that the father is to love the son. This ethical relationship is reduced to the relative as against the absolute relation to God. To the question, why?, Abraham has no other answer than that it is a trial and a temptation, which, as remarked above, is what makes it a unity of being for both God's sake and his own. These two are also correlative in ordinary usage. Thus when we see someone do something that doesn't conform with the universal, we say, 'He can hardly be doing that for the sake of God', meaning by this that he did it for his own sake. The paradox of faith has lost the intermediate term, i.e. the universal. On the one hand it contains the expression of extreme egoism (doing this dreadful deed for his own sake) and on the other the expression of the most absolute devotion (doing it for God's sake). Faith itself cannot be mediated into the universal, for in that case it would be cancelled. Faith is this paradox, and the single individual is quite unable to make himself intelligible to anyone. One might suppose the single individual could make himself understood to another individual who is in the same situation. Such a view would be unthinkable were it not that nowadays people try in so many ways to sneak their way into greatness. The one knight of faith simply cannot help the other. Either the single individual becomes a knight of faith himself by putting on the paradox, or he never becomes one. Partnership in these regions is quite unthinkable. If there is any more precise explanation of the idea behind the sacrifice of Isaac, it is one that the individual can only give to himself. And supposing one could settle, even with some exactitude, in universal terms, how to understand the case of Isaac (which would in any case be the most absurd self-contradiction, namely that the single individual who stands precisely outside the universal be brought in under universal categories, when he is expressly to act as the single individual outside the universal), the individual could still never be assured of [the truth of] this explanation by others, but only by himself as the single individual. So even if someone were so cowardly and base as to want to be a knight of faith on someone else's responsibility, he would never become one; for only the single individual becomes one, as the single individual, and this is the knight's greatness, as I can well understand without being party to it, since I lack courage; though also his terror, as I can understand even better.

As everyone knows, Luke 14.26 presents a remarkable teaching on the absolute duty to God: 'If any man come to me, and hate not his father, and mother, and wife, and children, and brethren, and sisters, yea, and his own life also, he cannot be my disciple.' This is a hard saying, who can bear to hear it? And for that reason it is heard very seldom. Yet this silence is only a futile evasion. The student of theology learns, however, that these words occur in the New Testament, and in one or another exegetical aid he finds the information that *misein* [to hate], both here and in some other passages, is used *per meiosin* [by adopting a weaker sense] to mean: *minus diligo* [love less], *posthabeo* [give less priority to], *non colo* [show no respect to], *nihil facio* [make nothing of].[76] The context in which these words occur seems, however, not to corroborate this tasteful explanation. For in the next verse [but one] there is a story about someone who plans to erect a tower but first makes some estimate of his capacity to do so, lest he be the object of ridicule later. The close link between this story and the verse quoted seems to suggest precisely that the words are to be taken in as terrifying a sense as possible in order that everyone should examine his own ability to erect the building.

If this pious and tender-minded exegete, who thinks he can smuggle Christianity into the world by haggling in this way, should succeed in convincing anyone that grammatically, linguistically, and *kata analogian* [by analogy] this was the meaning of the passage, then it is to be hoped that in so doing he also manages to convince the same person that Christianity is one of the most miserable things in the world. For the teaching which in one of its most lyrical outpourings, where the sense of its eternal validity swells up most strongly, has nothing to offer but a sounding phrase that signifies nothing and suggests only that one is to be less kind, less attentive, more indifferent; the teaching which, just as it seems to want to tell us something terrible, ends up in drivel rather than terror – that teaching is certainly not worth standing up for.

The words are terrible, but I feel sure they can be understood without the person who understands them necessarily having the courage to do as they say. And yet there must be honesty enough to admit what is there, to confess to its greatness even if one lacks the courage oneself. Anyone who manages that will not exclude himself from a share in the beautiful story, for in a way it contains a kind of comfort for the man who lacks courage to begin building the tower. But he must be honest and not pass off this lack of courage as humility, since on the contrary it is pride, while the courage of faith is the only humble courage.

One now sees readily that if the passage is to have any sense, it must be understood literally. It is God who demands absolute love. Anyone who, in demanding a person's love, thinks this must be proved by the latter's becoming lukewarm towards all that was hitherto dear to him, is not simply an egoist but a fool, and anyone demanding such a love would simultaneously sign his own death-warrant in so far as his life is bound up in this love he craves. A husband requires his wife to leave her father and mother, but were he to regard it as proof of her special love for him that for his sake she became a lukewarm, indolent daughter, etc., then he would be an idiot among idiots. Had he any notion of what love was, he would want to discover – and should he discover it see in this an assurance that his wife loved him more than any other in the kingdom – that she was perfect in her love as daughter and sister. So what would be considered a sign of egoism and stupidity in a person, one is supposed with the help of an exegete to regard as a worthy conception of the deity.

But how then *hate* them? I shall not take up the human love/hate distinction here, not because I have so much against it, since at least it is a passionate distinction, but it is egoistic and so does not fit here. If I regard the requirement as a paradox, on the other hand, then I understand it, i.e. understand it in the way one can understand a paradox. The absolute duty can then lead to what ethics would forbid, but it can by no means make the knight of faith have done with loving. This is shown by Abraham. The moment he is ready to sacrifice Isaac, the ethical expression for what he does is this: he hates Isaac. But if he actually hates Isaac he can be certain that God does not require this of him; for Cain and Abraham are not the same. Isaac he must love with all his soul. When God asks for Isaac, Abraham must if possible love him even more, and only then can he *sacrifice* him; for it is indeed this love of Isaac that in its paradoxical opposition to his love of God makes his act a sacrifice. But the distress and anguish in the paradox is that, humanly speaking, he is quite incapable of making himself understood. Only in the moment when his act is in absolute contradiction with his feeling, only then does he sacrifice Isaac, but the reality of his act is that in virtue of which he belongs to the universal, and there he is and remains a murderer.

Furthermore, the passage in Luke must be understood in such a way that one grasps that the knight of faith has no higher expression whatever of the universal (as the ethical) which can save him. Thus if we imagine the Church were to demand this sacrifice of one of its members, then all we have is a tragic hero. For qualitatively the idea of the Church is no different from that of the State, inasmuch as the individual can enter it by common mediation, and in so far as the individual has entered the paradox he does not arrive at the idea of the Church; he doesn't get out of the paradox either, but must find either his blessedness or his damnation inside it. An ecclesiastical hero expresses the universal in his deed, and no one in the Church, not even his father or mother, etc., will fail to understand him. But he is not the knight of faith, and has also a different answer from Abraham's; he doesn't say it is a trial or a temptation in which he is being tested.

One as a rule refrains from citing texts like the one in Luke. There is a fear of letting people loose, a fear that the worst will happen once the individual enjoys carrying on like an individual. Moreover living as the individual is thought to be the easiest thing of all, and it is the universal that people must be coerced into becoming. I can share neither this fear nor this opinion, and for the same reason. No person who has learned that to exist as the individual is the most terrifying thing of all will be afraid of saying it is the greatest. But then he mustn't say it in a way that makes his words a pitfall for somebody on the loose, but rather in a way that helps that person into the universal, even though his words can make some small allowance for greatness. The person who dares not mention such passages dares not mention Abraham either, and to think that existing as the individual is an easy enough matter implies a very dubious indirect admission with regard to oneself; for someone who really respects himself and is concerned for his own soul is assured of the fact that a person living under his own supervision in the world at large lives in greater austerity and seclusion than a maiden in her lady's bower. That there may be some who need coercion, who if given free rein would riot in selfish pleasure like unbridled beasts, is no doubt true, but one should show precisely by the fact that one knows how to speak with fear and trembling that one is not of their number. And out of respect for greatness one should indeed speak, lest it be forgotten for fear of the harm which surely won't arise if one speaks as one who knows it is the great, knows its terrors, and if one doesn't know these one doesn't know its greatness either.

Let us then consider more closely the distress and fear in the paradox of faith. The tragic hero renounces himself in order to express the universal; the knight of faith renounces the universal in order to be the particular. As mentioned, it all depends on how one is placed. Someone who believes it is a simple enough matter to be the individual can always be certain that he is not the knight of faith; for stragglers and vagrant geniuses are not men of faith. Faith's knight knows on the contrary that it is glorious to belong to the universal. He knows it is beautiful and benign to be the particular who translates himself into the universal, the one who so to speak makes a clear and elegant edition of himself, as immaculate as possible, and readable for all; he knows it is refreshing to become intelligible to oneself in the universal, so that he understands the universal and everyone who understands him understands the universal through him in turn, and both rejoice in the security of the universal. He knows it is beautiful to be born as the particular with the universal as his home, his friendly abode, which receives him straightaway with open arms when he wishes to stay there. But he also knows that higher up there winds a lonely path, narrow and steep; he knows it is terrible to be born in solitude outside the universal, to walk without meeting a single traveller. He knows very well where he is, and how he is related to men. Humanly speaking he is insane and cannot make himself understood to anyone. And yet 'insane' is the mildest expression for him. If he isn't viewed thus, he is a hypocrite and the higher up the path he climbs, the more dreadful a hypocrite he becomes.

The knight of faith knows it gives inspiration to surrender

oneself to the universal, that it takes courage to do so, but also that there is a certain security in it, just because it is for the universal; he knows it is glorious to be understood by every noble mind, and in such a way that even the beholder is thereby ennobled. This he knows and he feels as though bound, he could wish this was the task he had been set. Thus surely Abraham must have now and then wished that the task was to love Isaac in a way meet and fitting for a father, as all would understand and as would be remembered for all time; he must have wished his task was to sacrifice Isaac for the universal, so as to inspire fathers to illustrious deeds – and he must have been well nigh horrified by the thought that for him such wishes were merely temptations and must be treated as such; for he knew it was a solitary path he trod, and that he was doing nothing for the universal but only being tested and tried himself. Or what was it Abraham did for the universal? Let me speak humanly about it, really humanly! It takes him seventy years to get the son of his old age. What others get soon enough and have long joy of takes him seventy years. And why? Because he is being tested and tried. Is that not insanity? But Abraham believed, and only Sarah wavered and got him to take Hagar as his concubine – but for that reason he also had to drive Hagar away. He gets Isaac and now he is to be tried once again. He knew it was glorious to express the universal, glorious to live with Isaac. But this is not the task. He knew it would have been a kingly deed to sacrifice such a son for the universal, he himself would have found repose in that, and everyone would have 'reposed' in their praise of his deed, just as the vowel 'reposes' in its quiescent letter;[77] but this is not the task – he is being tried. That Roman general famous under the name of Cunctator halted the enemy by his delaying tactics,[78] yet what kind of delayer is Abraham by comparison? But he isn't saving the State. This is the sum of one hundred and thirty years. Who can bear it? Should his contemporaries – if they can be called that – not say: 'There is an eternal procrastinating with Abraham; when he finally gets a son – and that took long enough – he wants to sacrifice him; he must be demented; and if only he could explain why he wanted to do that, but no, it's always a "trial"'? Nor could

Abraham offer any further explanation, for his life is like a book put under divine seizure and which will never become *publici juris* [public property].

This is what is terrible. Anyone who doesn't see this can always be quite certain he is no knight of faith; but anyone who does see it will not deny that the step of even the most tried tragic hero goes like a dance compared with the slow and creeping progress of the knight of faith. And having seen it and realized he does not have the courage to understand it, he must at least have some idea of the wonderful glory achieved by that knight in becoming God's confidant, the Lord's friend, and – to speak really humanly – in addressing God in heaven as 'Thou', while even the tragic hero only addresses him in the third person.

The tragic hero is soon finished, his struggle is soon at an end; he makes the infinite movement and is now safe in the universal. But the knight of faith is kept awake, for he is under constant trial and can turn back in repentance to the universal at any moment, and this possibility can just as well be a temptation as the truth. Enlightenment as to which is something he can get from no one; otherwise he would be outside the paradox.

The knight of faith has therefore, first and foremost, the passion to concentrate the whole of the ethical that he violates in one single thing; he can be sure that he really loves Isaac with all his soul.* If he cannot be that, he is in a state of temptation. Next, he has the passion to evoke this certainty intact in a twinkling and in as fully valid a way as in the first instance. If

---

*I will explain once more the difference in the collision as between the tragic hero and the knight of faith. The tragic hero assures himself that the ethical obligation [to his son, daughter, etc.] is totally present in him by virtue of the fact that he transforms it into a desire. Thus Agamemnon can say: this is my proof that I am not violating my paternal obligation, that my duty [to Iphigenia] is my only wish. Here, then, desire and duty match one another. Happy my lot in life if my desire coincides with my duty, and conversely; and most people's task in life is exactly to stay under their obligation, and by their enthusiasm to transform it into their wish. The tragic hero renounces what he desires in order to accomplish his duty. For the knight of faith, wish and duty are also identical, but the knight of faith is required to give up both. So when renouncing in resignation what he desires he finds no repose; for it is after all his duty [that he is giving up]. If he stays under his obligation and keeps his desire he will not become the knight of faith: for the absolute duty requires precisely that he give up [the duty that is identical with the desire]. The tragic hero acquires a higher expression of duty, but not an absolute duty.

he cannot do this he doesn't get started, for then he must constantly start again from the beginning. The tragic hero, too, concentrates in one single thing the ethical that he teleologically violates, but in this thing he has resort to the universal. The knight of faith has only himself, and it is there the terrible lies. Most people let their ethical obligations last a day at a time, but then they never reach this passionate concentration, this energetic awareness. The tragic hero can in a sense be helped by the universal in acquiring these, but the knight of faith is alone about everything. The tragic hero acts and finds his point of rest in the universal, the knight of faith is kept in constant tension. Agamemnon gives up his claim to Iphigenia, thereby finds his point of rest in the universal, and now proceeds to give her in sacrifice. If Agamemnon had not made the movement, if in the decisive moment, instead of a passionate concentration, his soul had been lost in common chatter about his having several daughters, and *vielleicht das Ausserordentliche* [perhaps something extraordinary] could happen – then naturally he would not be a hero but a case for charity. Abraham has the hero's concentration too, even though in him it is much more difficult since he has no resort at all to the universal, but he makes one movement more through which he concentrates his soul back upon the marvel. If Abraham hadn't done that he would only have been an Agamemnon, provided it can be explained how his willingness to sacrifice Isaac can be justified other than by its benefiting the universal.

Whether the individual is now really in a state of temptation or a knight of faith, only the individual can decide. Still, it is possible on the basis of the paradox to construct certain criteria which even someone not in it can understand. The true knight of faith is always absolute isolation, the false knight is sectarian. The latter involves an attempt to leap off the narrow path of the paradox in order to become a tragic hero on the cheap. The tragic hero expresses the universal and sacrifices himself for it. The sectarian Master Jackel[79] has instead his private theatre, [i.e.] several good friends and companions who represent the universal about as well as the public witnesses in *The Golden Snuffbox*[80] represent justice. The knight of faith, on the other hand, is the paradox, he is the individual, absolutely nothing but the individual, without connections and complications. This is the terror that the puny sectarian cannot endure. Instead of learning from this that he is incapable of greatness and plainly admitting it, something I naturally cannot but approve since it is what I myself do, the poor wretch thinks he will achieve it by joining company with other poor wretches. But it won't at all work, no cheating is tolerated in the world of spirit. A dozen sectarians link arms, they know nothing at all of the lonely temptations in store for the knight of faith and which he dare not shun just because it would be more terrible still were he presumptuously to force his way forward. The sectarians deafen each other with their clang and clatter, hold dread at bay with their shrieks, and a whooping Sunday-outing[81] like this thinks it is storming heaven, believes it is following the same path as the knight of faith who, in cosmic isolation, hears never a voice but walks alone with his dreadful responsibility.

As for the knight of faith, he is assigned to himself alone, he has the pain of being unable to make himself intelligible to others but feels no vain desire to show others the way. The pain is the assurance, vain desires are unknown to him, his mind is too serious for that. The false knight readily betrays himself by this instantly acquired proficiency; he just doesn't grasp the point that if another individual is to walk the same path he has to be just as much the individual and is therefore in no need of guidance, least of all from one anxious to press his services on others. Here again, people unable to bear the martyrdom of unintelligibility jump off the path, and choose instead, conveniently enough, the world's admiration of their proficiency. The true knight of faith is a witness, never a teacher, and in this lies the deep humanity in him which is more worth than this foolish concern for others' weal and woe which is honoured under the name of sympathy, but which is really nothing but vanity. A person who wants only to be a witness confesses thereby that no one, not even the least, needs another person's sympathy, or is to be put down so another can raise himself up. But because what he himself won he did not win on the cheap, so neither does he sell it on the cheap; he is not so pitiable as to accept people's admiration and pay for it with silent contempt; he knows that whatever truly is great is available equally for all.

So either there is an absolute duty to God, and if so then it is the paradox described, that the single individual as the particular is higher than the universal and as the particular stands in an absolute relation to the absolute – or else faith has never existed because it has existed always; or else Abraham is done for; or else one must explain the passage in Luke 14 in the way that tasteful exegete did, and explain the corresponding passages likewise, and similar ones.[82]

PROBLEMA III

*Was it ethically defensible of Abraham to conceal his
purpose from Sarah, from Eleazar, from Isaac?*

The ethical is as such the universal; as the universal it is in turn
the disclosed. Seen as an immediate, no more than sensate and
psychic being, the individual is concealed. So his ethical task is
to unwrap himself from his concealment and become disclosed
in the universal. Thus whenever he wants to remain in concealment, he sins and is in a state of temptation, from which he can
emerge only by disclosing himself.

We find ourselves again at the same point. Unless there is a
concealment which has its basis in the single individual's being
higher than the universal, then Abraham's conduct cannot be
defended, since he disregarded the intermediate ethical considerations. If, however, there is such a concealment, then we
face the paradox, which cannot be mediated, just because it is
based on the single individual's being, in his particularity, higher
than the universal, and it is precisely the universal that is the
mediation. The Hegelian philosophy assumes there is no justified
concealment, no justified incommensurability. It is therefore
consistent in its requirement of disclosure,[83] but it isn't quite fair
and square in wanting to regard Abraham as the father of faith
and to speak about faith. For faith is not the first immediacy but
a later one. The first immediacy is the aesthetic,[84] and here the
Hegelian philosophy may well be right. But faith is not the
aesthetic, or if it is, then faith has never existed just because it
has existed always.

It will be best here to look at the whole matter in a purely
aesthetic way and for that purpose embark on an aesthetic
inquiry, which I would ask the reader for the time being to enter
wholeheartedly into, while I for my part will adapt my presentation accordingly. The category I would like to examine a little
more closely is that of the *interesting*, a category that especially
today (just because we live *in discrimine rerum* [at a turning-point

in human affairs]) has acquired great importance, for really it is the category of crisis. Therefore one should not, as sometimes happens, when one has been oneself enamoured of it *pro virili* [with all one's strength], disdain the category because it has passed one by; but neither should one be too greedy for it, for what is certain is that to become of interest, for one's life to be interesting, has nothing to do with what you can turn your hand to but is a fateful privilege which, like every privilege in the world of spirit, can only be purchased in deep pain. Thus Socrates was the most interesting person that has lived, his life the most interesting that has been led, but that existence was allotted to him by the deity, and since he had to work for it he was no stranger to trouble and pain. Taking such an existence in vain ill-becomes someone who takes life seriously, and yet such attempts are nowadays not infrequently observed. The category of the interesting is, moreover, a borderline one, it marks the boundary between the aesthetic and the ethical.[85] For that reason in our inquiry we must be constantly glancing over into the territory of ethics, while to give our inquiries weight the problem must be grasped with genuine aesthetic feeling.[86] These days ethics rarely considers such things. The reason is supposed to be that there is no room for them in the System. But then doing so in monographs should be all right; and besides, if one doesn't want to be long-winded about it one can achieve the same results by being brief, so long as one has the predicate in one's power; for a predicate or two can reveal a whole world. Is there no room in the System for little words like these?

Aristotle says in his immortal *Poetics*: '*duo men oun tou muthou meri, peri taut' esti, peripeteia kai anagnorisis*' (cf. Ch. 11) ['... indeed two parts in the myth, namely sudden change of fortune [the reverse (on which the plot of a tragedy turns)]] and recognition, concern these things']. Naturally only the second feature, *anagnorisis*, recognition, concerns me here. Whenever there is recognition there is *eo ipso* a question of prior concealment. Just as the recognition is the resolving factor, or the element of relaxation in the life of drama, so is concealment the element of tension. What Aristotle says earlier in the same chapter in respect of the consequences for the worth of tragedy of the question whether *peripeteia* and *anagnorisis* clash, as well as of the 'single' and 'double' recognition,[87] I cannot go into here, even though the sincerity and quiet absorption of Aristotle's discussion have an inevitable attraction for one long since tired of the superficial omniscience of the synopticists. A general observation must suffice. In Greek tragedy concealment (and therefore recognition) is an epic survival based on a fate in which the dramatic action disappears from view, and from which it acquires its obscure and enigmatic origin. This is why the effect produced by a Greek tragedy bears a resemblance to the impression given by a marble statue that lacks the power of the eye. Greek tragedy is blind. Hence it takes a certain abstraction to appreciate it. A son murders his father, but not until later learns it is his father.[88] A sister is about to sacrifice her brother, but at the decisive moment discovers that is who it is.[89] Tragedy of this nature is less apt to interest our *reflective* age. Modern drama has given up the idea of Fate, has in dramatic respects emancipated itself; it observes, it looks in upon itself, takes fate up into its dramatic consciousness. Concealment and disclosure then become the hero's free act, for which he is responsible.

Recognition and concealment are also an essential part of modern drama. It would take us too far to give examples. I am courteous enough to assume that everyone in this so aesthetically voluptuous age, so potent and aroused that conception occurs as easily as with the partridge which, Aristotle says, needs only to hear the voice of the cock or its flight overhead[90] – to assume that at the mere sound of the word 'concealment' everyone can easily shake a dozen romances and comedies from his sleeve. I can therefore be brief and offer straightaway a fairly broad observation. If the person doing the hiding, i.e. the one who puts the dramatic yeast into the play, hides something nonsensical, we have comedy. But if the concealer is related to the idea, he may come close to being a tragic hero. To give just one example of the comic. A man puts on make-up and wears a wig. The same man wants to have success with the fair sex, and is sure enough of conquests with the help of the make-up and wig, which there is no doubt make him irresistible. He captures a girl and is on the pinnacle of joy. But now for the point. If he can admit his deception, will he not lose *all* of his powers of fascination once he is revealed as a quite ordinary, in fact even bald-headed male? Doesn't he have to lose the loved one again? Concealment is his free action, for which aesthetics holds him responsible. But that discipline is no friend of bald hypocrites, and will leave him to the mercy of our laughter. Let that suffice as a hint of what I mean, since we cannot include comedy in the terms of this investigation.

My procedure here must be to let concealment pass dialectically between aesthetics and ethics, for the point is to show how absolutely different the paradox and aesthetic concealment are from one another.

A few examples. A girl is secretly in love, though neither party has openly confessed its love to the other. Her parents force her to marry another (she may even be motivated out of considerations of duty). She obeys. She hides her love 'so as not to make the other unhappy, and no one will ever know what she suffers'. – Or a young lad is in a position, just by dropping one word, to possess the object of his craving and restless dreams. But that little word will compromise, yes, even, who knows, ruin an entire family. He nobly chooses to stay in concealment, 'the girl must never know, so that she can perhaps find happiness with another'. What a pity that these two, both concealed from their respective loved ones, are also concealed from one another! For otherwise a remarkable higher unity might have been brought about. – Their concealment is a free act, for which even aesthetically they are responsible. However, aesthetics is a respectful and sentimental discipline which knows more ways of fixing things than any assistant house-manager. So what does it do? It does everything possible for the lovers. By means of a coincidence the respective partners in the projected marriages get wind of the other party's noble decision. Explanations follow. They get each other and as a bonus the rank of real heroes as well; for notwithstanding they have had no time even to sleep on their heroic resolutions, aesthetics sees it as if they had bravely fought for their goal over many years. For aesthetics doesn't bother much about time; it goes just as quickly whether in jest or earnest.

But ethics knows nothing either of this coincidence or this

sentimentality. Nor does it have such a rapid concept of time. Thus the matter acquires a different complexion. You can't argue with ethics, because it uses pure categories. It doesn't appeal to experience, which of all laughable things is perhaps the most laughable and, far from making a man wise, if he knows nothing higher it will sooner make him mad. Ethics has no coincidence, so no explanations follow; it doesn't flirt with thoughts of dignity, it puts an enormous burden of responsibility on the hero's frail shoulders; it condemns as presumptuous his thought of wanting to play providence in his action, but also condemns him for wanting to do likewise with his suffering. It enjoins the belief in reality and the courage to contend with all its tribulations, rather than with those bloodless sufferings he has taken on himself by his own responsibility; it warns against putting faith in the calculating shrewdness of reason, more treacherous than the oracles of the ancients. It warns against all misplaced magnanimity. Let reality decide the occasion, that is the time to show courage. But then ethics, too, will offer every possible assistance. If something deeper had been stirring in those two, however, if there had been a seriousness to see the task, to set about it, then no doubt something would have come of them. But ethics cannot help them. Ethics is offended because they are keeping a secret from it, a secret they have incurred on their own responsibility.

Thus aesthetics called for concealment and rewarded it. Ethics called for disclosure and punished concealment.

Sometimes, however, even aesthetics calls for disclosure. When the hero held captive in the aesthetic illusion believes he can save another by his silence, aesthetics calls for silence and rewards it. But when the hero's action involves interfering in another person's life, it calls for disclosure. Now I am talking of the tragic hero. Consider for a moment Euripides's *Iphigenia in Aulis*. Agamemnon is about to sacrifice Iphigenia. Now aesthetics calls for Agamemnon's silence, in so far as it would be unworthy of the hero to seek another's consolation, just as he should keep it quiet as long as possible for the women's sake. On the other hand the hero, to be that, has also to be tested in the terrible temptation incurred by the tears of Clytemnestra and Iphigenia.

What does aesthetics do? It has a way out; it has an old servant standing by who discloses everything to Clytemnestra.[91] And now everything is as it should be.

Ethics, however, has no coincidence, and no old servant standing by. The aesthetic idea contradicts itself as soon as it is applied in reality. Ethics therefore demands disclosure. The tragic hero demonstrates exactly this ethical courage by, not himself being captive to the aesthetic illusion, taking it upon himself to tell Iphigenia her fate. In this the tragic hero is the beloved son of ethics, in whom she is well pleased. If he remains silent, it may be because by doing so he makes it easier for others, or it could also be because it makes it easier for himself. But the tragic hero knows he is free of the latter incentive. In keeping silent here he would be assuming responsibility as an individual, inasmuch as he is impervious to any argument from outside. But this, as tragic hero, he cannot do; for it is just in so far as he continues to express the universal that ethics loves him. His heroic action requires courage, but part of that courage is that he shirks no argument. Now tears, certainly, are a terrible *argumentum ad hominem*,[92] and there are no doubt those whom nothing else touches but who can still be stirred by tears. The play lets Iphigenia weep, in fact like Jephthah's daughter she should have been allowed two months to weep, not in solitude but at her father's feet, to use all her art 'which is but tears', and twine herself instead of the olive branch about his knees (cf. v. 1224).[93]

Aesthetics required disclosure but availed itself of a coincidence; ethics required disclosure and found satisfaction in the tragic hero.

For all the strictness of the ethical requirement of disclosure, it cannot be denied that secrecy and silence, as determinants of inner feeling, really make for greatness in a man. When Amor leaves Psyche he says to her, 'You will give birth to a child who will be divine if you say nothing, but human if you betray the secret.' The tragic hero, the darling of ethics, is a purely human being, and he is someone I can understand, someone all of whose undertakings are in the open. If I go further I always run up against the paradox, the divine and the demonic; for silence is both of these. It is the demon's lure, and the more silent one keeps the more terrible the demon becomes; but silence is also divinity's communion with the individual.

Before coming back to the story of Abraham, however, I would like to present some poetic personages. By exercising the power of dialectic over them I shall keep them at extremes, and by waving the scourge of despair over them I should prevent them from standing still, so that in their anguish they might perhaps bring something or other to light.*

Aristotle tells in his *Politics* of a political disturbance in Delphi, arising from a marriage. *The bridegroom, for whom the augurs*[95] *had predicted a misfortune as a result of his forthcoming marriage, at the crucial moment, when he is to fetch the bride, suddenly changes his plans* – he won't go through with the wedding. That is all I need.† In Delphi this surely did not pass off without tears. If a poet took it up he could doubtless count on arousing sympathy. Is it not terrible that the love so often excluded in life should here also be deprived of the aid of heaven? Isn't the old proverb that marriages are made in heaven here put to shame? Usually it is the trials and tribulations of finitude which, like evil spirits,

---

* These movements and attitudes could also be handled aesthetically. But I leave it open how far faith and the life of belief in general can be handled in that way. I will only – since I always like to thank those to whom I owe something – express my gratitude to Lessing for the few hints of a Christian drama to be found in his *Hamburgische Dramaturgie.*[96] But he has focused on the purely divine side of that life (the consummated victory), and has therefore despaired. Perhaps if he had paid more attention to the human side he would have come to a different conclusion. (*Theologia viatorum* [wayfarer's theology].) What he says is undeniably very brief, partly evasive, but as I am always very glad of the chance of Lessing's company I seize on it immediately. Lessing was not just one of the most erudite minds Germany has produced; he was not just unusually exact in his learning, so that one can safely rely on him and his autopsy without fear of being tricked by inaccurate and concocted quotations, half-understood phrases taken from unreliable compendia, or of being put off-balance by a foolish advertising of novelties that the ancients have stated far better; he had in addition a most unusual gift for explaining what he himself had understood. There he stopped. Nowadays one goes further and explains more than one has understood.

† According to Aristotle the course of the catastrophe is as follows. In order to avenge itself, the [bride's] family plants a vase from the temple among the bridegroom's household belongings and he is condemned as a temple-robber. But this is immaterial, for the question is not whether the family is clever or stupid in the manner of its taking revenge; the family is of only theoretical interest in as much as it impinges on the dialectic of the hero. Besides, there is fatefulness enough in the fact that, though intending to avoid the danger by not marrying, he plunges right into it, together with the fact that his life comes into twofold contact with the divine, first in the utterance of the augur and second by his being condemned as a temple-robber.

would separate the lovers, while love itself has heaven on its side
and this holy alliance overwhelms all foes. Here it is heaven itself
that separates what heaven, after all, has joined together. Who
would have guessed? The young bride least of all. A moment
earlier she was sitting in her room in all her beauty, and the
sweet young maids had adorned her with such care that they
would be prepared to justify their handiwork before the whole
world, that it gave them more than happiness, it even made
them envious – yes, even happy that they couldn't be even more
envious, since she could not have been more beautiful. Sitting
there alone in her room she was then transfigured from one
beauty to another; for all that a woman's art could accomplish
had been turned virtuously to the embellishment of virtue. But
there still lacked something the young girl had not dreamed of,
a veil, finer, lighter, and yet more concealing than the one in
which the young maids had enveloped her, a bridal gown no
maid had knowledge of or could help her with, even the bride
herself did not know how to put it on. It was an unseen, friendly
influence which takes satisfaction in adorning a bride and wraps
itself around her without her knowledge, for all she saw was the
bridegroom walking by on his way to the temple. She saw the
door close after him, and she became even more calm and
blissful, for she knew that he now belonged to her more than
ever. The temple door opened, he stepped out, but demurely she
turned her gaze down and so did not see that his face was
troubled. Yet he saw that heaven must be jealous of the bride's
loveliness and of his good fortune. The temple door opened, the
young maids saw the bridegroom step out, but they did not see
that his face was troubled, for they were busy about bringing the
bride. Then she came forward in all her maidenly modesty, and
yet like a mistress surrounded by her *cortège* of young maids of
honour, who curtsied before her as a young maid always curtsies
before a bride. Thus at the head of her lovely troupe she stood
and waited – it was but a moment, for the temple was close by
– and the bridegroom came, but he passed by her door.

But here I break off. I am not a poet, I only practise dialectics.
One should note first of all that it is at the crucial moment that
the hero learns what is in store, so he is pure and blameless,

hasn't bound himself irresponsibly to the loved one. Second,
it is a divine utterance he has before him, or rather against
him,[96] so he is not ruled like those feeble lovers and sweethearts
by conceit. Further, it goes without saying that this utterance
makes him just as unhappy as the bride, indeed rather more
so since after all he is the occasion. True, the augurs only
predicted a misfortune for *him*, but the question is whether the
misfortune is not of such a nature as to affect also their marital
happiness. So what is he to do? (1) Is he to remain silent and
get married and think 'Perhaps the misfortune won't come right
away, and anyway I have been true to my love and not afraid
to make myself unhappy; but I must remain silent, otherwise
even the brief moment is lost.' This sounds plausible but is in
fact by no means so, for in this he insults the girl. By keeping
silent he has in a way made her guilty, for had she known the
truth she would never have given her consent to such a union.
So in the hour of need he will have to bear not only the misfortune but also the responsibility for not having said anything,
as well as her righteous anger at his not having said anything.
(2) Is he to remain silent and not get married? In that case he
must enter into a deception in which he annihilates himself in
his relation to her. Aesthetics might approve of this. The
catastrophe could then be fashioned as in the real story except
that at the last moment there would be explanations, though
too late since aesthetically it will be necessary to let him die,
unless that discipline can see its way to revoking the fateful
prophecy. Yet, noble as this conduct may be, it involves an insult
to the girl and the reality of her love. (3) Is he to speak? Naturally
one mustn't forget that our hero is a little too poetic for the
giving up of his love to have no importance except as an unsuccessful business venture. If he speaks, then the whole thing
becomes an unfortunate love-story in the vein of Axel and
Valborg.[97] They will be a couple whom heaven itself puts
asunder. Nevertheless in the present case this separation is to
be conceived somewhat differently, since it, too, is also the result
of the free acts of the individuals. For what is so very difficult
with the dialectic in this case is that the misfortune is to affect
only him. These two, then, do not find a common expression

of their suffering, as do Axel and Valborg, whom heaven
separates equally from each other because they are equally close
to each other.* If that were the case here, a way out could be
found. For since heaven uses no visible power to separate them,
but leaves it to them, one could well imagine that they ended
united in defiance of heaven together with its misfortune.

Ethics, however, will require him to speak. The essence of
his valour in that case is to be found in his giving up his aesthetic
high-mindedness, which here could hardly be thought to
contain any admixture of the vanity connected with concealment, since it must be clear to him that he still makes the girl
unhappy. The reality of this heroism is based, however, on its
having had and cancelled its presupposition [that he genuinely
loved her and kept quiet for her sake and not his – translator's
addition]; for otherwise we would get heroes enough, particularly in our own time which has acquired a matchless
proficiency in the forgery that does the highest by skipping over
what lies in between.

But why this sketch if I nevertheless come no further than
the tragic hero? Because it might still throw light on the paradox.
That all depends on our hero's relationship to that utterance

* Here one might trace the dialectic movements in a different direction. Heaven
predicts a personal misfortune due to the marriage, so he could just as well give
up the marriage yet needn't give up the girl on that account, but live in a romantic
relationship with her which was more than satisfactory for the lovers. This,
however, amounts to insulting the girl, for in his love for her he doesn't express
the universal, and it was the task both of the poet and of the ethicist to defend
marriage. On the whole, were poetry to attend to the religious aspect and to the
inner feeling of its characters, it would command themes of much greater
importance than those it now occupies itself with. Here is the story poetry is
repeatedly giving us: a man is stuck with a girl he once loved, or maybe never
really loved because he has now seen another who is the ideal. A man makes
mistakes in life, it was the right street but the wrong house, for on the second
floor just over the way lives the ideal – that's what people consider the proper
subject of poetry. A lover makes a mistake, he saw his loved one by candlelight
and thought she had dark hair, but look!, on closer inspection she was blonde
– however, the sister, there's the ideal. That's what people think poetry is about.
In my view any such man is an impudent fool who can be unbearable enough
in life but should be instantly booed off the stage when he tries to put on airs
in poetry. Only the clash of passion against passion provides a poetic collision,
not this rummaging about in the particulars of the same passion. In the Middle
Ages, for example, when a girl has fallen in love and then been convinced that
earthly love is a sin and prefers a heavenly love, here we have a poetic collision;
and the girl too is poetic, for her life is in the idea.

of the augur's, which in one way or another is going to decide
the course of his life. Is this utterance *publici juris* [public
property] or is it a *privatissimum* [private matter]? The scene
is laid in Greece; an augur's utterance is intelligible to all – I
don't mean just in the sense that the individual can grasp the
content lexically, but that the individual can understand that
what an augur is conveying to him is a decision of heaven's.
So the augur's utterance is intelligible not just to the hero but
to everyone and results in no private relation to the divine. Turn
where he will, what was prophesied will happen, and neither
by doing anything nor by refraining from doing anything will
he come into a closer relationship with the divine, become an
object either of divine mercy or of divine wrath. The outcome
will be as understandable to anyone as to the hero, and there is
no secret writing that only the hero can read. So should he want
to speak he can perfectly well do so, for he can make himself
understood; and if he wants to remain silent it is because he
wants, by virtue of being the single individual, to be higher than
the universal, wants to delude himself with all manner of phan-
tasies about how she will soon forget this sorrow, etc. On the
other hand, if the will of heaven had not been announced to him
by an augur, if it had been made known to him in some quite
private way, if it had placed itself in a quite private relationship
to him, then we are with the paradox – supposing there is such
a thing (since my reflections here have the form of a dilemma)
– then he could not speak however much he might wish to. He
would not enjoy his own silence but suffer the pain, yet for him
just this would be the assurance he needed that he did right. So
the reason for his silence would not be a wish to place himself
as the single individual in an absolute relation to the *universal*,
but to be placed as the single individual in an absolute relationship to the *absolute*. In this, so far as I can tell, he would also be
able to find repose, whereas the requirements of the ethical
would be constantly disturbing his high-minded silence. One
only wishes that aesthetics might try to start where for so many
years it has ended, with the illusion of high-mindedness. As soon
as it did so it would work hand in hand with religion, for that
is the only power capable of rescuing the aesthetic from its

conflict with the ethical. Queen Elizabeth sacrifices to the State her love for Essex by signing his death-warrant.[98] That was a deed of heroism, even if some private resentment had a hand in it because he hadn't sent her the ring. We know that he did send it, but it was held back through the malice of some lady-in-waiting. Elizabeth is said, *ni fallor* [if I am not mistaken], to have been informed of this, and sat for ten days with one finger in her mouth, biting it without saying a word, and then she died. That would be something for a poet who knew how to wrench open the mouth; otherwise it would be of use at best to a ballet master, with whom nowadays the poet no doubt too often confuses himself.

I now want to follow this by a sketch along the lines of the demonic. For this I shall use the legend of *Agnete and the Merman*.[99] The merman is a seducer who rises up from concealment in the depths, and in wild desire grasps and breaks the innocent flower standing in all its charm by the shore, pensively bending its head to the ocean's roar. That is what the poets have so far made of it. Let us make a change. The merman was a seducer. He has called out to Agnete, with his smooth talk has coaxed from her her secret thoughts. She has found in the merman what she was seeking, what she gazed down to find in the depths of the sea. Agnete is willing to follow him down. The merman has taken her into his arms, Agnete twines hers about his neck trustingly and with all her soul she abandons herself to the stronger one. He is already at the sea-edge, bending over the water to dive down with his prey. Then Agnete looks at him again, not fearfully, not questioningly, not proud of her good luck, not intoxicated with desire, but in absolute faith, with absolute humility, like the humble flower she deemed herself to be; with absolute confidence she entrusts to him her entire fate. – And look! The ocean roars no more, its wild voice is stilled, nature's passion – which is the merman's strength – deserts him, the sea becomes dead calm. And still Agnete is looking at him in this way. Then the merman collapses, he is unable to resist the power of innocence, his element becomes unfaithful to him, he cannot seduce Agnete. He leads her home again, he explains to her that he only wanted to show her how beautiful the sea is when it is calm, and Agnete believes him.

Then he turns back alone, and the ocean rages, but more wildly still rages the merman's despair. He can seduce Agnete, he can seduce hundreds of Agnetes, he can charm any girl – but Agnete has triumphed and the merman has lost her. Only as his prize can she become his; he cannot belong faithfully to any girl, for he is only a merman. I have allowed myself a slight modification* in the merman. In fact I have slightly altered Agnete too. In the legend Agnete is by no means guiltless – and in general it is nonsense and sheer coquetry as well as an insult to the female sex to imagine a seduction where the girl is in no way, in no way at all, to blame. In the legend Agnete is, to modernize my expression somewhat, a woman who hankers for 'the interesting', and one such can always be certain there is a merman in the offing; for mermen keep a weather-eye open for the likes of these and they make for them like a shark for its prey. It is therefore very foolish to suppose (or is it a rumour spread abroad by the merman?) that so-called refinement protects a girl from seduction. No, life is more just and fair; there is only one means of protection, it is innocence.

We will now give the merman a human consciousness, and let his being a merman indicate a human pre-existence in the

* There is still another way of treating this legend. The merman does not want to seduce Agnete, even though he has seduced many previously. He is no longer a merman, or is if you will a pitiable merman who has now already for some time been sitting sorrowfully on the sea-bed. However, he knows (as indeed the legend has it[100]) that he can be saved by an innocent girl's love. But he has a bad conscience about girls and dare not approach them. Then he sees Agnete. Already, many times, as he lay hidden in the reeds, he has seen her walking along the shore. Her beauty, her quiet self-possession captivate him; but his soul is filled with sadness, no wild desire rages there. And when the merman blends his sigh with the whispering of the reeds she turns her ear towards it. Then she stands still and falls into reverie, more delectable than any woman and yet beautiful as an angel of deliverance, who inspired the merman with confidence. The merman plucks up courage, he approaches Agnete, he wins her love, he hopes for his deliverance. But Agnete was no quiet girl, she was in fact very taken with the roaring of the ocean and what pleased her about the sad sighing by the sea was that it made the roar in her breast grow stronger. She would be off and away, rush wildly out into the infinite with the merman, whom she loves – so she eggs the merman on. She scorned his humility and now the pride reawakens. And the sea roars and the waves foam, and the merman embraces Agnete, and dives with her into the depths. Never had he been so wild, never so full of desire; for with this girl he had hoped for his deliverance. Before long he became tired of Agnete, but her body was never found; for she became a mermaid, who tempted men with her songs.

consequences of which his life has become entangled. There is
nothing to prevent his being a hero; for the step he now takes
is reconciliatory. He is saved by Agnete, the seducer is crushed,
he has bowed to the power of innocence, he can never seduce
again. But immediately two powers claim control of him:
repentance [alone] and repentance with Agnete. If repentance
alone takes possession of him he remains concealed, if
repentance and Agnete take possession of him he is disclosed.

Now in so far as repentance alone grips the merman and he
remains concealed, then he must certainly make Agnete unhappy; for Agnete loved him in all her innocence, she believed
him that moment when even to her he seemed changed, however well he concealed it, and said he only wanted to show her
the beautiful calm of the sea. However, as far as passion is concerned, the merman himself becomes even more unhappy; for
he loved Agnete with a multiplicity of passions and has a new
guilt to bear besides. The demonic side of repentance will now
no doubt explain to him that this is precisely his punishment,
and the more it torments him the better.

If he gives in to this demonic possibility, he may make one
more attempt to save Agnete, in the way one can in a sense save
someone by resort to evil. He knows Agnete loves him. If he can
only tear this love away from her she will in a way be saved. But
how to do that? The merman has too much sense to reckon that
a candid confession will arouse her disgust. Then perhaps he will
try to arouse all dark passions in her, scorn her, mock her, hold
her love up to ridicule, if possible stir up her pride. He will spare
himself no torment, for this is the deep contradiction in the
demonic and in a sense there dwells infinitely more good in a
demonic than in a superficial person. The more selfish Agnete
is, the more easily she will be deceived (only those with very little
experience think it easy to deceive innocence, life is very profound
and it is the astute who find it easiest to trick one another), but
all the more terribly the merman will suffer. The more ingeni-
ously contrived his deception the less will Agnete bashfully hide
her own pain from him; she will use every means, not without
effect, not, that is, to shake him loose but to torment him.

By means of the demonic the merman would thus aspire to

be the single individual who as the particular is higher than the universal. The demonic has that same property as the divine, that the individual can enter into an absolute relationship to it. This is the analogue, the counterpart to the paradox we are discussing. It therefore bears a certain resemblance to it that can prove misleading. Thus the merman apparently has the proof of the justification of his silence that it is because of it that he suffers all his pain. However, there is no doubt that he can speak. So he can be a tragic hero, to my mind a tragic hero on the grand scale, if he does speak. Perhaps only few will understand what the grandeur consists in.* He will then have the courage to free himself of all self-deception about being able to make Agnete happy by his art; he will have the courage to crush Agnete, humanly speaking. Here I will just add a psychological observation. The more selfish we make Agnete, the more effective the self-deception will be, indeed it is not inconceivable that with his demonic astuteness a merman might in reality not only have, humanly speaking, saved Agnete but brought something exceptional out of her. A demon knows how to torture powers out of even the weakest person, and in his way he can have the best intentions towards a human being.

The merman stands at a dialectical extremity. If he is saved from the demonic side of repentance two paths are possible. He can hold himself back, remain in hiding, but not depend on his astuteness. In that case he does not come as the single individual into an absolute relation to the demonic, but finds repose in the counter-paradox that the divine will save Agnete. (This is how the movement would have been made in the Middle Ages, for on its conception the merman has obviously dedicated

* Aesthetics sometimes treats a similar theme with its usual captiousness. The merman is saved through Agnete and all ends in a happy marriage. A happy marriage! Very handy, to be sure. On the other hand if ethics is to give the wedding speech I imagine things would go differently. Aesthetics throws the cloak of love over the merman and so everything is forgotten. It is also rash enough to suppose that things happen at a wedding as they do at an auction, where everything is sold in the condition it is in when it comes under the hammer. All it cares for is that the lovers get one another, the rest is of no concern. If only it could see what happens afterwards! But it hasn't time for that, straightaway it is in full swing again snapping together another couple. Aesthetics is the most faithless of all sciences. Anyone who has truly loved it will in a way become unhappy; while anyone who has never done so is and will remain a *pecus* [ox, or blockhead].

himself to the monastery.[101]) Or else he can be saved through
Agnete. Now this must not be understood as meaning that
Agnete's love might save him from being a seducer in the future
(that is an aesthetic rescue attempt, which always avoids the
main issue, namely the continuity in the merman's life); in that
respect he is already saved. He will be saved in so far as he
is disclosed. So he marries Agnete. But he must still resort to
the paradox. For when through his own guilt the individual
has come out of the universal, he can only return to it on the
strength of having come, as the particular, into an absolute
relation to the absolute. Here I will insert a comment which takes
us further than anything that has been said anywhere in the
foregoing.* Sin is not the first immediacy, sin is a later immediacy.
In sin the individual is already in terms of the demonic paradox
higher than the universal, because it is a contradiction on the
part of the universal to want to impose itself on someone who
lacks the *conditio sine qua non* [the necessary condition].[102]
Should philosophy, amongst its other conceits, imagine that
someone might actually want to follow its precepts in practice,
a curious comedy would emerge. An ethics that ignores sin is an
altogether futile discipline, but once it postulates sin it has *eo ipso*
[thereby] gone beyond itself. Philosophy tells us that the immediate is to be superseded [*ophævet*, German *aufgehoben*]. True
enough, but what is not true is that sin, any more than faith,
is without further ado the immediate.

Everything goes smoothly so long as I move in these spheres,
but in fact not even what is said here helps to explain Abraham.
He did not become the single individual through sin; on the
contrary he was that righteous man who is God's chosen. So
any analogy with Abraham will only surface after the individual
has become capable of accomplishing the universal, and now
the paradox is repeated.

I can therefore understand the movements of the merman,

* Up to this point I have carefully avoided all consideration of the question of
sin and its reality. Everything has been centred on Abraham, and he can still
be reached with the categories of immediacy, at least so far as I can understand
him. But once sin makes its appearance ethics comes to grief precisely on the
question of repentance. Repentance is the highest ethical expression but for that
very reason the most profound ethical self-contradiction.

but I cannot understand Abraham. It is to realize the universal
that the merman has recourse to the paradox. If he stays hidden
and dedicates himself to all the torments of repentance, he
becomes a demon, and as such is brought to nothing. If he stays
hidden but entertains no clever thoughts about being able to
extricate Agnete at the cost of his own torment in the bondage
of repentance, he will no doubt find peace but is lost to the world.
If he discloses himself, lets himself be saved through Agnete,
then he is the greatest human being I can imagine. It is only
aesthetics which irresponsibly thinks it can praise the power
of love by letting the lost man be loved by an innocent girl and
saved thereby. Only aesthetics mistakes what it sees and
thinks the girl rather than the merman is the hero. So the
merman cannot belong to Agnete before, after making the
infinite movement of repentance, he has made one more movement, that on the strength of the absurd. His own strength
suffices for the movement of repentance, but it calls for
absolutely all his energies, and it is therefore impossible for him
by his own strength to return and grasp reality. If one lacks
sufficient passion to make either movement, when one scrimps
through life, repenting a little and thinking the rest will take
care of itself, one has given up living in the idea once and for
all, and then it is very easy to reach, and help others reach,
the highest; i.e. delude oneself and others with the notion that
the world of spirit is like *Gnavspil* [a card game], where everyone
cheats. So one can amuse oneself by reflecting how strange it
is that just in an age when everyone can reach the highest there
should be such widespread doubt about the immortality of the
soul; since even someone who has only, but genuinely, made
the movement of infinity can scarcely be called a doubter. The
conclusions of passion are the only reliable, i.e. the only
convincing, ones. Fortunately life is in this case more kindly,
more faithful, than the wise would have it. It excludes no one,
not even the humblest; it tricks nobody, for in the world of spirit
the only people who are tricked are those who trick themselves.
It is the general opinion, and as far as I dare be my own judge,
also my own, that entering the monastery is not the highest.
But I by no means believe on that account that the fact that

nobody goes into monasteries today means that we are all greater than those profound and earnest souls who found repose there. How many people are there now with the passion to think this thought and then judge themselves honestly? The very idea of thus taking time on one's conscience, of giving conscience time to search out with its sleepless perseverance every secret thought, so that unless one is making the movement every instant on the strength of what is noblest and most holy in a human being one can discover with anguish and horror,* and call forth by anguish itself if by nothing else, the dark passions which after all lie concealed in every human life, whereas living in society with others one so easily forgets, so easily avoids, is in so many ways held above all this, gets the chance to start again – this very idea, grasped with decent respect, I would have thought could in itself chasten many an individual in this age of ours which thinks it has already reached the highest. Yet such things worry people little in this age that thinks it has reached the heights, though no age has fallen so much victim to the comic than ours. Indeed it is hard to grasp why it hasn't already given birth, by a *generatio æquivoca* [spontaneous generation], to its hero, that demon who will stage without scruple that horrifying play that reduces the whole age to laughter and to unconsciousness of the fact that it is laughing at itself. Indeed what more is life worth than to be laughed at when people have already reached the highest by the time they are twenty? And yet what higher movement has the age come up with since people gave up entering monasteries? Is it not a contemptible worldliness, a circumspection and pusillanimity that sits at the head of the table, cravenly making people think they have reached the highest, and even slyly dissuading them from trying anything less? A person who has made the monastery movement has only one movement to go, that of the absurd. How many nowadays understand what the absurd is, how

---

*This is not credited in our serious age, and yet remarkably enough even in the typically flightier and less consistently reflective age of paganism the two representatives of the Greek *gnothi sauton* [know thyself] way of thought have, each in his own manner, intimated that if one probes one's own depths what one uncovers is first and foremost the disposition to evil. I need hardly remark that I am thinking of Pythagoras and Socrates.

many live in such a way as to have renounced or gained every-thing, how many are even simply honest enough to know what they are and what they can and cannot do? And is it not true that if there are such, they are mostly to be found among the less educated and in part among women? Just as a demonic person always reveals himself without understanding himself, our age betrays its own defects in a kind of clairvoyance, for it is always calling for the comical. If that was really what it needed then perhaps the theatre would need a new play in which someone's dying for love was treated as comedy. Or would it not be better for our age if that were really to happen, if it were actually to witness such an occurrence, so that it might acquire the courage to believe in the power of spirit, the courage to stop abjectly stifling its better impulses, stop jealously stifling them in others – with laughter? Does the age really need a ridiculous *Erscheinung* [appearance, show] of an enthusiast in order to have something to laugh at? Or does it not rather need such an enthusiastic figure in reality to remind it of what it has forgotten?

If one wants a scenario along similar lines but more moving because the passion of repentance is not awakened, one can use a story from the Book of Tobit.[103] The young Tobias wishes to marry Sarah, the daughter of Raguel and Edna. But the girl is surrounded in tragedy. She has been betrothed to seven men all of whom have died in the bride's house. For my scenario this is a flaw in the story, since there is something almost irresistibly comical in the thought of a girl's seven vain attempts to get married, although so near success, as near as a student who fails his finals seven times. The Book of Tobit places the accent elsewhere and that makes the high number important and in a certain sense even contributes to the tragic effect. It enhances the young Tobias's high-mindedness, partly because he is his parents' only son (6.14), partly because the deterrent obtrudes the more strongly. So this feature must be omitted. Sarah, then, is a girl who has never been in love, who still nurtures a young girl's notion of bliss, her immense mortgage in life, her *Vollmachtbrief zum Glücke* [authorization for happi-ness][104] – to love a man with all her heart. And yet she is the most unhappy of all, for she knows that the evil demon that

loves her will kill the bridegroom on the wedding night. I have
read of much sorrow, but I doubt if anywhere there is a sorrow
as deep as that residing in the life of that girl. Nevertheless when
the misfortune comes from outside there is a certain consolation.
If life fails to bring a person what would make him happy, it
is still a comfort that he could have received it. But the unfathomable sorrow which no time can disperse, no time heal,
is to know that it would be no use even if life were to do everything! A Greek author conceals so infinitely much in his crude
naïveté when he says: *'pantos gar oudeis Erota epfugen i feuksetai
mechri an kallos i kai ofthalmoi Bleposin'* ['... for certainly no one
has yet altogether escaped love, and none shall so long as there
is beauty and eyes to see'] (cf. *Longi Pastoralia*).[105] Many a girl
has been made unhappy in love, but she *became* unhappy; Sarah
was so before she became it. It is hard enough that one should
not find the one to whom one can devote oneself, but *unspeakably*
hard to be unable to devote oneself. A young girl surrenders
herself to someone and then she is said no longer to be free,
but Sarah was never free and yet never surrendered herself to
anyone. It is hard enough that a girl should surrender herself
to someone and be deceived by her love, but Sarah was deceived
before she surrendered herself. What world of sorrow is not contained in what follows, when at length Tobias wishes to marry
Sarah! What wedding-rites, what preparations! No girl was
ever cheated as Sarah. She was cheated of the most blessed of
all things, the absolute wealth which even the poorest girl
possesses, cheated of the secure, unbounded, unfettered, unbridled self-surrender of devotion. For first there had to be the
ritual of purification by placing the heart of a fish and its liver
on glowing embers. And what a mother's leave-taking of the
daughter who, just as she herself has been cheated of everything,
must also cheat her own mother of *her* most beautiful possession.
One just reads the narrative.[106] Edna prepared the chamber and
brought Sarah into it and wept, and she received the tears of her
daughter – and said to her, 'My child, take heart. The Lord of
heaven and earth may exchange your sorrow for joy. Daughter,
take heart.' And now the moment for the wedding. We read on,
if we can for tears: 'But when the door was shut and they were

together, Tobias rose from the bed and said, "Rise up, sister, and we will pray that the Lord may have mercy on us" ' (8.4).

Were a poet to read this story and use it, I wager a hundred to one he would place all the emphasis on the young Tobias. The heroism of being willing to risk his life in such obvious danger, of which the narrative reminds us once again, for the morning after the wedding Raguel says to Edna: 'Send one of the maids to see if he is still alive, so that, if not, we can bury him and no one will know it' (cf. 8.13) – this heroism would have been the theme for the poet. I venture to propose another. Certainly Tobias acted gallantly, resolutely, and chivalrously, but any man who lacks courage to do that is a milksop who knows neither what love is nor what it is to be a man, nor what is worth living for. He has not even grasped the little mystery that it is better to give than to receive, and has no inkling of what the great mystery is, namely that it is much harder to receive than to give, that is if one has had the courage to go without and did not prove a coward in the hour of need. No, Sarah is the heroine. Her I would like to draw close to as I have drawn close to no other girl, or been tempted to draw close in thought to anyone of whom I have read. For what love for God it takes to want to be healed when one has been crippled from the start for no fault of one's own, an unsuccessful specimen of humanity from the very beginning! What ethical maturity to take on the responsibility of allowing the loved one such an act of daring! What humility before another person! What faith in God that in the next instant she should not hate the man to whom she owed everything!

Let Sarah be a man and the demonic will not be far away. A proud and noble nature can endure everything, but one thing it cannot endure, it cannot endure pity. Pity implies an indignity that for such a person can only be inflicted from above, for in himself he can never become an object of pity. If he has sinned he can endure the punishment without despairing, but to be singled out from his mother's womb as an object of pity, a sweet fragrance in pity's nostrils, that he cannot bear. Pity has a curious dialectic; one moment it calls for guilt, the next it wants to do away with it, and so to be predestined to pity is the more dreadful the greater the individual's misfortune lies in the direction of the spiritual. But no guilt attaches to Sarah, she is thrown as a prey to every suffering and on top of that has to be tortured by human sympathy, for even I who admire her more than Tobias loves her, even I cannot mention her name without exclaiming 'The poor girl!' Let a man take Sarah's place, let him know that if he is to love a girl an infernal spirit will come and murder her on the wedding night, then he would certainly be likely to choose the demonic, shut himself up in himself and say in his heart, as does the demonic nature, 'Thanks, I am no friend of ceremony and fuss, I don't at all insist on the pleasures of love, I can just as well be a Bluebeard who gets his pleasure seeing girls die on their wedding night.' One generally hears very little about the demonic, in spite of this territory's having a peculiarly valid claim to discovery in our time, and notwithstanding that once he knows how to establish a certain rapport with the demon an observer can, at least in some respect or other, use almost anyone as an example. In this respect Shakespeare is and will always remain a hero. That horrid demon, the most demonic figure Shakespeare ever portrayed, and did so incomparably, Gloucester (later Richard III), what made him a demon? Obviously that he could not endure the pity that had been piled on him from childhood. His monologue in the first act of *King Richard III* is worth more than all moral systems, none of which bears a hint of the terrors of existence and of their nature.

> I, that am rudely stamped, and want love's majesty
> To strut before a wanton ambling nymph;
> I, that am curtailed of this fair proportion,
> Cheated of feature by dissembling nature,
> Deformed, unfinished, sent before my time
> Into this breathing world scarce half made up,
> And that so lamely and unfashionable
> That dogs bark at me as I halt by them ...[107]

Natures like Gloucester's cannot be saved by mediating them into an idea of society. Ethics really only makes fun of them, just as it would make a mockery of Sarah if it were to say to her, 'Why don't you express the universal and get married?'

Such natures are aboriginally in the paradox, and they are by no means less perfect than others; it is only that they are either damned in the demonic paradox or delivered in the divine. Now people have been pleased to think from time immemorial that witches, gnomes, trolls, etc. are misshapen creatures, and it is undeniable that we all have a tendency when we see a misshapen person directly to link this idea with that of moral perversion. But what colossal injustice! It should really be the other way around. It is life itself that has corrupted them, as a stepmother makes degenerates of her stepchildren.[108] To be put outside the universal from the start, by nature or by historical circumstance, that is the beginning of the demonic, and the individual can hardly be blamed for that. So Cumberland's Jew is also a demon notwithstanding his beneficence.[109] Thus the demonic can also express itself in contempt for men, a contempt which it should nevertheless be noted does not make the demonic person himself act contemptuously; on the contrary his strength is his knowledge that he is better than all who pass judgement on him. – On all such matters the poets should be the first to make a stir. God knows what books our young versifiers are reading these days! Their studies are no doubt confined to learning rhymes by rote. Heaven knows what importance they have in life! Just now I couldn't honestly tell you whether they are good for anything but to give us edifying proof of the immortality of the soul, to the extent at least that one can safely say of them what Baggesen says of the city's poet, Kildevalle: 'if he is immortal then we all are'.[110] – What has been said here about Sarah, almost in the style of a poetic production, appealing therefore in effect only to the imagination, finds its full significance if out of psychological interest one probes the meaning of the old saying: *'nullum unquam exstitit magnum ingenium sine aliqua dementia'* ['there was never great genius without some madness'].[111] For the *dementia* here is the genius's suffering in life, is the expression, if I may say so, of divine jealousy, while genius itself is the mark of divine favour. Thus the genius is disorientated from the start in relation to the universal and put into relation to the paradox, whether, in despair over his own limitation, which in his own eyes turns his omnipotence into impotence, he seeks a demonic reassurance

and therefore will not admit the limitation to either God or man,
or he reassures himself religiously in love for the divine. There
are psychological topics here to which it seems to me one could
happily devote a lifetime, and yet we so rarely hear a word about
them. How is madness related to genius? Can the one be construc-
ted out of the other? In what sense and to what extent is the
genius master of his own madness? For it goes without saying
that to some degree he is indeed its master, otherwise he would
really be mad. Performing such observations requires, however,
a high order of ingenuity as well as love, since performing
observations on people of superior talent is extremely difficult.
If one bears this in mind in reading some of those authors most
celebrated for their genius, it is conceivable that one might just,
once in a while, though only with great effort, find out something.

I would like to consider one more case of an individual
wanting to save the universal by his concealment and silence.
I shall take the legend of *Faust*. Faust is a doubter,* an apostate

* If one would rather not use a doubter, a similar figure would do. An ironist, for
example, whose sharp eye has taken radical measure of the ludicrousness of life,
who through a secret understanding with the forces of life ascertains what the
patient needs. He knows he commands the power of laughter; should he wish to
wield it he would be sure of victory and, what is even better, of his happiness. He
knows some voice is going to raise itself against him, but also that he himself is
the stronger; he knows people can still be brought for a moment to appear serious
– but also that, privately, they long to laugh with him; he knows that it is still possible
to bring a woman for a moment to hold up her fan before her eyes when she speaks,
but he also knows that behind the fan she is laughing, he knows the fan is not
completely opaque, he knows one can make invisible inscriptions on it, he knows
that when a woman strikes at him with the fan it is because she has understood
him, he knows infallibly how laughter creeps into a person and dwells there secretly,
and how once lodged there it lies in ambush and waits. Let us suppose such an
Aristophanes, such a Voltaire, slightly altered, for he is also of a sympathetic nature,
he loves life, loves people, and knows that even if a young, saved generation might
benefit from the rebuke of laughter, in his own age for many it would mean rack
and ruin. So he keeps silent and as far as possible forgets to laugh himself. But does
he dare keep silent? Perhaps many will fail to see the difficulty I am referring to.
They will probably consider it admirably high-minded of him to keep silent. That
is not at all what I think. I believe that if any such person has not the magnanimity
to keep silent he is a traitor to life. So I require this magnanimity of him. But if he
has it he dares to keep silent. Ethics is a dangerous science and it may well have
been out of purely ethical considerations that Aristophanes decided to let laughter
pass judgement on his misguided age. Aesthetic magnanimity cannot help. Its
account has no credit column for the taking of such risks. If he is silent he must
enter the paradox. – Still another scenario: suppose, for example, someone is in
possession of an explanation of a public hero's life, but one that explains it in a
deplorable light, and yet a whole generation rests secure in this hero and has no
suspicion of anything of the sort.

of the spirit who goes the way of the flesh. This is how the poets see it, and although it is repeated over and over again that every age has its Faust, poets still doggedly follow one another down this same beaten path. Let us make a slight change. Faust is a doubter *kat'eksochen* [in an eminent sense]; but he has a sympathetic nature. Even in Goethe's understanding of Faust I miss a deeper psychological insight into the secret conversations which doubt has with itself. Nowadays, when indeed all have experienced doubt, no poet has as yet made a move in this direction. I could think of offering them Royal Securities to write on, to put down 'all' they have experienced in this regard – for it is unlikely that what they have to say will take more than the left-hand margin.

Only when one turns Faust back in on himself in this way – only then can the doubt appear poetically, only then does he himself genuinely discover in reality all its sufferings. Then he knows it is spirit that sustains life, but he also knows that the security and happiness people live in are not supported by the power of spirit but can be readily explained as unreflective bliss. As a doubter, as *the* doubter, he is above all that, and if someone wants to deceive him into supposing that he had put doubt behind him, he easily sees through that. One who has made a movement in the world of spirit, hence an infinite movement, can tell at once from the spoken line whether the speaker is a man of experience or a Münchhausen. What a Tamerlane could do with his Huns,[112] Faust knows he can do with his doubt – frighten people out of their wits, make the very world shake under their feet, send people scattering in every direction, and cause the cry of alarm to sound from every quarter. And if he does that he is still not a Tamerlane, for having the warrant of thought he is in a sense authorized to act in this way. But Faust has a sympathetic nature, he loves life, his soul knows no envy, he sees he would be unable to prevent the landslide that would no doubt be set in motion, he has no wish for Herostratic honour[113] – he remains silent, he hides his doubt in his soul more assiduously than the girl the fruit of her sinful love beneath her heart, he tries as well as he can to walk in step with others, but as far as what goes on inside him, that he consumes internally and in this way he makes himself a sacrifice to the universal.

Sometimes, when some eccentric raises the whirlwind of doubt, one hears the complaint: 'If only he had kept quiet.' Faust too represents this notion. Anyone with any idea of what it means to live on spirit knows also what the hunger of doubt means, and that the doubter hungers just as much for the daily bread of life as for the sustenance of spirit. Even though all the pain Faust suffers can be a fairly good argument for its not being pride that possesses him, I shall nevertheless avail myself of a small precautionary device which is easy enough for me to come by, who, just as Gregory of Rimini was called *tortor infantium* because he subscribed to the damnation of infants, might be tempted to call myself *tortor heroum*[114] – I am very inventive when it comes to torturing heroes. Faust sees Marguerite – not after he has chosen the life of pleasure, since my Faust doesn't choose pleasure at all – he sees Marguerite not in Mephistopheles's concave mirror but in all her lovable innocence, and because his soul has preserved its love for humankind he can also very well fall in love with her. But he is a doubter, his doubt has destroyed reality for him. So ideal is my Faust that he is not one of those scientific doubters who doubt for an hour every term at the lectern but can otherwise do anything, as indeed they do without the help of spirit or on its strength. He is a doubter, and the doubter hungers as much for his daily slice of joy as for the nourishment of spirit. But still he stays true to his decision, is silent, and talks to no one of his doubt, nor to Marguerite of his love.

It goes without saying that Faust is too ideal a figure to be satisfied with the tattle that if he spoke he would only set a more general discussion in motion, or that the whole affair would blow over without consequences, or perhaps this or perhaps that. (Here, as will be obvious to any poet, lies the dormant comedy in our scenario, bringing Faust into ironical relation to those slapstick fools who nowadays chase after doubt, produce an external argument, e.g. a doctor's certificate, to show that they have really doubted, or take an oath that they have doubted everything, or else prove it by the fact that on their journey they met up with a doubter – those express couriers and sprint-experts in the world of spirit who in all haste gather a little hint of doubt from this person and a little hint of faith from that, and then *wirtschafte* [do business] as best they may depending on whether the congregation wants fine sand or coarse sand.[115]) Faust is too ideal a figure to walk about in slippers. No one who lacks an infinite passion is ideal and anyone who does have an infinite passion has long since saved his soul from such rubbish. He is silent so as to offer himself – or else he talks, well knowing that he will put everything into confusion.

He is silent, so ethics condemns him. It says: 'You must acknowledge the universal, and you do that by speaking, and you dare not take pity on the universal.' This is something one should not forget when one sometimes judges a doubter severely for speaking. I myself am not inclined to judge such conduct leniently, but here as everywhere it is a question of the movements occurring properly. If things go wrong, then a doubter, even if by speaking he should bring all manner of misfortune upon the world, would still be far preferable to these miserable sweet-tooths who try a taste of everything and would cure doubt without being acquainted with it, and are therefore as a rule the immediate cause of outbreaks of ungoverned and unmanageable doubt. – If he speaks he confuses everything, for if nothing happens he only finds that out afterwards, and the consequence can be of no help either in the moment of acting or in questions of responsibility.

If he is silent on his own responsibility, he may indeed be acting magnanimously, but to his other pains there is added a little temptation. The universal will be forever plaguing him and saying, 'You should have spoken, how can you be certain that it wasn't after all some hidden pride that prompted your decision?'

If on the other hand the doubter can be the single individual who as the particular stands in an absolute relation to the absolute, then he receives authorization for his silence. But then he must make guilt of his doubt. But then he is in the paradox. But then his doubt is cured, even though he can acquire another.

Even the New Testament would approve such a silence. There are passages in the New Testament even extolling irony, so long as it is the better side that it is used to conceal. However, this movement is just as much a movement of irony as any other movement based on subjectivity's being higher than reality. This is something no one nowadays wants to know; generally people want to know no more about irony than Hegel has said about it, though curiously enough he had rather little understanding of it and indeed bore a grudge against it which our age finds good reason not to give up, seeing that for it irony is simply something it must guard itself against. The Sermon on the Mount says: 'But thou, when thou fastest, anoint thine head, and wash thy face; that thou appear not unto men to fast'.[116] The passage gives clear testimony to subjectivity's incommensurability with reality, indeed even to its having the right to deceive. If only those people who wander about these days with vague talk of the idea of the congregation would read the New Testament, they might come upon other ideas.[117]

But now Abraham. How did he act? For I have not forgotten, and the reader may now be pleased to recall, that this was the point to which the whole preceding discussion was intended to lead. Not to make Abraham more intelligible thereby, but in order that his unintelligibility might be seen more in the round,[118] for, as I have said, I cannot understand Abraham, I can only admire him. It was also mentioned that none of the stages described contained an analogue of Abraham, they were elaborated only so as to indicate, from the point of view of their own sphere, the boundary of the unknown land by the points of discrepancy. If there should be any question of an analogy here it would have to be the paradox of sin, but that again belongs to another sphere and cannot explain Abraham, and is itself far easier to explain than Abraham.

So Abraham did not speak. He spoke neither to Sarah, to Eleazar, nor to Isaac. He passed over these three ethical authorities. Because for Abraham the ethical had no higher expression than that of family life.

Aesthetics allowed, in fact demanded, silence of the individual when by remaining silent he could save another. This is already enough to show that Abraham does not lie within the circumference of aesthetics. His silence is not at all to save Isaac, as in general the whole task of sacrificing Isaac for his own and God's sake is an outrage aesthetically. Aesthetics can well understand that I sacrifice myself, but not that I should sacrifice another for my own sake. The aesthetic hero was silent. Ethics condemned him, however, because it was on the strength of his accidental particularity that he remained silent. His human prescience was what determined that he should be silent. This ethics cannot forgive. All such human insight is only an illusion. Ethics demands an infinite movement which requires disclosure. So the aesthetic hero can indeed speak but will not.

The genuine tragic hero sacrifices himself and everything he has for the universal; his action, every emotion in him belongs to the universal, he is revealed, and in this disclosure he is the beloved son of ethics. This does not apply to Abraham. He does nothing for the universal and he is concealed.

We are now at the paradox. Either the individual as the particular can stand in an absolute relation to the absolute, and then the ethical is not the highest, or Abraham is done for, he is neither a tragic hero nor an aesthetic hero.

Here again the paradox might seem the easiest and most convenient thing of all. However, I must repeat that anyone who remains convinced of that is not the knight of faith, for distress and anguish are the only justification conceivable, even though they cannot be conceived in general, for if they could the paradox would be cancelled.

Abraham is silent – but he *cannot* speak, therein lies the distress and anguish. For if when I speak I cannot make myself understood, I do not speak even if I keep talking without stop day and night. This is the case with Abraham. He can say what he will, but there is one thing he cannot say and since he cannot say it, i.e. say it in a way that another understands it, he does not speak. The relief of speech is that it translates me into the universal. Now Abraham can say the most beautiful things any language can muster about how he loves Isaac. But this is not what he has in mind, that being the deeper thought that he would have to sacrifice Isaac because it was a trial. This no one can understand, and so no one can but misunderstand the former. Of this distress the tragic hero knows nothing. In the first place he has the consolation that all counter-arguments

have been done justice to, that he has been able to give
Clytemnestra, Iphigenia, Achilles, the Chorus, every living
being, every voice from the heart of humankind, every
intelligent, every anxious, every accusing, every compassionate
thought an opportunity to stand up against him. He can be
sure that all that it is possible to say against him has been said,
unsparingly, mercilessly – and to contend with the whole world
is a comfort, but to contend with oneself dreadful. – He need
have no fear of having overlooked something, of later having
to cry out like King Edward IV at the news of the death of
Clarence:

> Who sued to me for him? Who, in my wrath,
> Kneeled at my feet and bid me be advised?
> Who spoke of brotherhood? Who spoke of love?[119]

The tragic hero knows nothing of the terrible responsibility
of solitude. Moreover, he has the comfort of being able to weep
and wail with Clytemnestra and Iphigenia – and sobbing and
crying give relief, while groans that cannot be uttered are
torture. Agamemnon can rally himself quickly to the certainty
that he will act, and he therefore still has time to bring comfort
and courage. This Abraham cannot do. When his heart is
stirred, when his words would convey a blessed consolation for
the whole world, he dare not console, for would not Sarah,
would not Eleazar, would not Isaac say to him, 'Why do you
want to do this, you can after all refrain'? And if in his distress
he should want to unburden his feelings and embrace everything dear to him before taking the final step, then this might
have the most frightful consequence that Sarah, that Eleazar,
that Isaac would be offended in him and believe him a hypocrite.
Talk he cannot, he speaks no human language. Though he
himself understood all the tongues of the world, though the
loved ones understood them too – he still could not talk – he
speaks a divine tongue – he 'speaks with tongues'.[120]

This distress I can well understand. I can admire Abraham.
I have no fear that anyone should be tempted by this story to
want irresponsibly to be the single individual. But I also confess
that I myself lack the courage for that, and that I would gladly

renounce any prospect of coming further if only it were possible for me to come that far, however late in the day. Abraham can refrain at any moment, he can repent the whole thing as a temptation. Then he can speak, then all will understand him – but then he is no longer Abraham.

Abraham *cannot* speak. What would explain everything, that it is a trial – though note, one in which the ethical is the temptation – is something he cannot say (i.e. in a way that can be understood). Anyone so placed is an emigrant from the sphere of the universal. And yet what comes next he is even less able to say. For, as was made sufficiently clear earlier, Abraham makes two movements. He makes the infinite movement of resignation and gives up his claim to Isaac, something no one can understand because it is a private undertaking. But then he further makes, and at every moment is making, the movement of faith. This is his comfort. For he says, 'Nevertheless it won't happen, or if it does the Lord will give me a new Isaac on the strength of the absurd.' The tragic hero does at least get to the end of the story. Iphigenia bows to her father's decision, she herself makes the infinite movement of resignation and they now understand one another. She is able to understand Agamemnon because his undertaking expresses the universal. If on the other hand Agamemnon were to say to her, 'Even though the deity demands you as a sacrifice, it's still possible that he didn't – on the strength of the absurd', he would instantly become unintelligible to her. If he could say it on the strength of human calculation, then Iphigenia would surely understand him. But that would mean that Agamemnon had not made the infinite movement of resignation, and then he would not be a hero, and then the seer's utterance is just a traveller's tale and the whole incident a piece of vaudeville.

So Abraham did not speak. Only one word of his has been preserved, his only reply to Isaac, which we can take to be sufficient evidence that he had not spoken previously. Isaac asks Abraham where the lamb is for the burnt offering. 'And Abraham said: My son, God will provide himself a lamb for a burnt offering.'[121]

This last word of Abraham's I shall consider here a little more closely. If it had not occurred the whole incident would lack something. If it had been a different word everything might dissolve in confusion.

I have often pondered on how far a tragic hero, whether suffering or action provides the consummation of his heroism, ought to have a final remark. So far as I can see it depends on what sphere of life he belongs to, on the extent to which his life has intellectual significance, on how far his suffering or action stand in relation to spirit.

It goes without saying that at the moment of consummation the tragic hero, like anyone else, is capable of a few words, even a few appropriate words. But the question is whether it is appropriate for him to say them. If the significance of his life consists in an outward act, then he has nothing to say, since everything he says is essentially idle chat which can only weaken the impact he makes, while the rites of tragedy require on the contrary that he fulfil his task in silence, whether in action or suffering. So as not to go too far afield I shall simply draw on our nearest example. If Agamemnon himself, and not Calchas [the seer], had had to draw the knife on Iphigenia he would only have demeaned himself by wanting to say a few words at the last moment. Everyone knew the significance of his deed, the whole process of piety, pity, feeling, and tears was done with, and besides, his life had no relation to spirit, i.e. he was not a teacher or a witness to the spirit. If on the other hand the significance of the hero's life tends towards spirit, the lack of a remark will weaken the impact he makes. It is not something appropriate he should be saying, not some bit of rhetoric, but something that will convey that he is consummating himself in the decisive moment. An intellectual tragic hero of this kind should allow himself what people often aspire to frivolously, namely having and keeping the last word. We expect of him the same exalted bearing as becomes any tragic hero, but on top of that we expect some word. So if an intellectual tragic hero consummates his heroism in suffering (in death), in this final word he will become immortal before he dies, while the ordinary tragic hero only becomes immortal after his death.

Socrates can be used as an example. He was an intellectual

tragic hero. He hears his death-sentence. That instant he dies. Unless you grasp that it requires all the strength of spirit to die, that the hero always dies before his death, you will not come particularly far in your observations on life. So as a hero Socrates is required to stay calm and at ease, but as an intellectual hero he is required to have sufficient spiritual strength at the final moment to fulfil himself. So he cannot, like the ordinary tragic hero, concentrate on keeping himself face to face with death; he has to make this latter movement so quickly that in the same instant he is consciously above that conflict and continues to assert himself. Had Socrates been silent in the crisis of death he would have weakened the effect of his life, aroused a suspicion that the resilience of irony was not, in him, a primitive strength, but only a game whose flexibility he had to exploit in the decisive moment, according to an opposite standard, pathetically to sustain himself.*

What I have been briefly hinting at here doesn't really apply to Abraham, to the extent that one supposes one might find by analogy some appropriate word for Abraham; but it applies to the extent that one sees the necessity of Abraham's fulfilling himself at the final moment not by drawing the knife silently but by having something to say, seeing that as the father of faith he has absolute significance in terms of spirit. As to *what* he is to say, I can form no idea in advance. Once he has said it I can no doubt understand it, even in a sense understand Abraham *in* what is said, yet without thereby coming any nearer him than in the foregoing. If we'd had no remark from Socrates I could have put myself into his position and made one, and if I couldn't do that myself, a poet would have managed. But no poet can reach Abraham.

Before going on to consider Abraham's last word more closely, I must first draw attention to the difficulty of Abraham's coming

* Which of Socrates's remarks is to be regarded as the decisive one can be a matter of controversy, since Socrates has been in so many ways poetically volatilized by Plato. I suggest the following: the death-sentence is announced to him, that instant he dies and fulfils himself in the famous rejoinder that he was surprised to have been condemned with a majority of three votes.[122] He could have found no more ironic jest in some market-place flippancy or fool's inanity than in this comment on the death-sentence which condemns him from life itself.

to say anything at all. The distress and anguish in the paradox consisted, as explained above, precisely in the silence; Abraham cannot speak.* To that extent then it is self-contradictory to demand that he should speak, unless one wants him out of the paradox again, so that in the decisive moment he suspends it, whereby he ceases to be Abraham and brings to naught all that went before. Were Abraham, at the decisive moment, to say to Isaac, 'It is you who are to be sacrificed', this would only be a weakness. For if he could speak at all he should have done so long before, and the weakness then consists in his not having the maturity of spirit and concentration to imagine the whole of the pain beforehand but having pushed some of it aside so that the actual pain proves greater than the imagined one. Besides, with talk of this kind he would fall out of the paradox, and if he really wanted to talk to Isaac he would have to transform his own situation into that of a temptation. Otherwise, after all, he could say nothing and if he does so transform his situation he isn't even a tragic hero.

Nevertheless a last word of Abraham's *has* been preserved, and so far as I can understand the paradox I can also understand Abraham's total presence in that word. First and foremost he doesn't say anything, and that is his way of saying what he has to say. His answer to Isaac has the form of irony, for it is always irony to say something and yet not say it. Isaac asks Abraham because he assumes Abraham knows. Now if Abraham had replied, 'I know nothing', he would have uttered an untruth. He cannot say anything, since what he knows he cannot say. So he replies, 'My son, God will provide himself a lamb for a burnt offering.' Here one sees the double movement in Abraham's soul, as it has been described in the foregoing. Had Abraham simply renounced his claim to Isaac and done no more, he would have uttered an untruth. He knows that God demands the sacrifice of Isaac, and he knows that precisely at this moment he himself is ready to sacrifice him. So, after having made this

---

*In so far as there is any question of an analogy [here], the circumstances of the death of Pythagoras provide one. In his last moments Pythagoras had to consummate the silence he had always maintained, and so he *said*, 'It's better to be killed than to speak.' cf. Diogenes, 8th Bk, § 39.[123]

movement Abraham has at every instant been performing the next, making the movement on the strength of the absurd. To that extent he utters no untruth, for on the strength of the absurd it is after all possible that God might do something quite different. He utters no untruth then, but neither does he say anything, for he speaks in a foreign tongue. This becomes still more obvious when we consider that it was Abraham himself who was to sacrifice Isaac. If the task had been a different one, if the Lord had commanded Abraham to take Isaac out on the mountain in Moriah, and then let his own lightning strike Isaac and take him as a sacrifice in that way, Abraham would in a straightforward sense be right to talk as enigmatically as he did, for in that case he himself could not have known what would happen. But as the task is given to Abraham, it is he who must act, so he must know at the decisive moment what he is about to do, and accordingly must know that Isaac is to be sacrificed. If he doesn't definitely know that, he hasn't made the infinite movement of resignation, in which case his words are not indeed untrue, but then at the same time he is very far from being Abraham, he is less significant than a tragic hero, he is in fact an irresolute man who can resolve to do neither one thing nor the other, and who will therefore always come to talk in riddles. But such a *Haesitator* [waverer] is simply a parody of the knight of faith.

Here too it can appear that one can understand Abraham, but only as one understands the paradox. For my part I can in a way understand Abraham, but I see very well that I lack the courage to speak in this way, as much as I lack the courage to act like Abraham. But I do not at all say that what he did is inconsiderable on that account, since on the contrary it is the one and only marvel.

And what did contemporaries think of the tragic hero? That he was great, and they looked up to him. And that noble assembly of worthies, the jury that every generation appoints to pass judgement on its predecessor, came to the same verdict. But none could understand Abraham. And yet think what he achieved! To remain true to his love. But he who loves God has no need of tears, needs no admiration, and forgets his

suffering in love, indeed forgets so completely that afterwards
not the least hint of his pain would remain were God himself
not to remember it; for God sees in secret and knows the distress
and counts the tears and forgets nothing.

So either there is a paradox, that the single individual as the
particular stands in an absolute relation to the absolute, or
Abraham is done for.

EPILOGUE

Once when the spice market in Holland was a little slack, the merchants had some cargoes dumped at sea to force up the price. That was a pardonable, perhaps necessary, stratagem. Is it something similar we need in the world of spirit? Are we so convinced of having reached the heights that there is nothing left but piously to believe we still haven't come that far, so as at least to have something to fill the time with? Is it this kind of trick of self-deception the present generation needs, is it to a virtuosity in this it should be educated, or has it not already perfected itself sufficiently in the art of self-deception? Or is what it needs not rather an honest seriousness which fearlessly and incorruptibly calls attention to the tasks, an honest seriousness that lovingly fences the tasks about, which does not frighten people into wanting to dash precipitately to the heights, but keeps the tasks young and beautiful and charming to behold, and inviting to all, yet hard too and an inspiration to noble minds, since noble natures are only inspired by difficulty? Whatever one generation learns from another, it can never learn from a predecessor the genuinely human factor. In this respect every generation begins afresh, has no task other than that of any previous generation, and comes no further, provided the latter didn't shirk its task and deceive itself. This authentically human factor is passion, in which the one generation also fully understands the other and understands itself. Thus no generation has learned from another how to love, no generation can begin other than at the beginning, the task of no later generation is shorter than its predecessor's, and if someone, unlike the previous generation, is unwilling to stay with love but wants to go further, then that is simply idle and foolish talk.

But the highest passion in a human being is faith, and here no generation begins other than where its predecessor did, every generation begins from the beginning, the succeeding generation comes no further than the previous one, provided the latter was true to its task and didn't betray it. That this sounds wearying is not of course for the generation to say, for it is indeed the generation that has the task and it has nothing to do with the fact that the previous generation had the same task, unless that particular generation or the individuals in it presumed to occupy the position to which only the spirit that governs the world, and which has the endurance not to grow weary, is entitled. If that is the kind of thing the generation begins to do, it is perverted, and what wonder then if the whole of existence should look perverted to it? For surely no one has found life more perverted than the tailor in the fairy-tale who got to heaven in his lifetime and from there looked down on the world.[124] So long as the generation only worries about its task, which is the highest it can attain to, it cannot grow weary. That task is always enough for a human lifetime. When children on holiday get through all their games by noon and then ask impatiently, 'Can't anyone think of a new game?', does this show that they are more developed and advanced than children of the same or a previous generation who could make the games they already know last the whole day? Or does it not rather show that those children lack what I would call the good-natured seriousness that belongs to play?

Faith is the highest passion in a human being. Many in every generation may not come that far, but none comes further. Whether there are also many who do not discover it in our own age I leave open. I can only refer to my own experience, that of one who makes no secret of the fact that he has far to go, yet without therefore wishing to deceive either himself or what is great by reducing this latter to a triviality, to a children's disease which one must hope to get over as soon as possible. But life has tasks enough, even for one who fails to come as far as faith, and when he loves these honestly life won't be a waste either, even if it can never compare with that of those who had a sense of the highest and grasped it. But anyone who comes to faith (whether he be greatly talented or simple-minded makes no difference) won't remain at a standstill there. Indeed he would be shocked if anyone said this to him. Just as the lover would be indignant if someone said he had come to a standstill in his love, for he would reply, 'I'm by no means standing still in my love, for I have my life in it.' And yet he too doesn't come any further, not to anything else. For when he finds that out he has another explanation.

'One must go further, one must go further.' This need to go on is of ancient standing. Heraclitus the 'obscure' who reposited his thoughts in his writings and his writings in the Temple of Diana (for his thoughts had been his armour in life, which he therefore hung up in the temple of the goddess), the obscure Heraclitus has said, 'One can never walk through the same river twice.'* The obscure Heraclitus had a disciple who didn't remain standing there but went further and added, 'One cannot do it even once.'† Poor Heraclitus to have such a disciple![125] This improvement changed the Heraclitian principle into an Eleatic doctrine denying movement, and yet all that disciple wanted was to be a disciple of Heraclitus who went further, not back to what Heraclitus had abandoned.

* '*Chai potamou roi apeikadzon ta onta legei hos dis es ton auton potamon ouk embaiis.*' cf. Plato's *Cratyllus* §402. Ast. 3rd B. Pag. 158.
† cf. Tennemann *Gesch. d. Philos.* Ister B. Pag. 220.

NOTES

1. Quoted from J. G. Hamann, *Werke* III, p. 190. While engaged in war with Gabii, Tarquinius Superbus (an early king of Rome) had his son flee to Gabii under the pretence that he had been mistreated by his father. The inhabitants made him their military leader, and by striking off the heads of the tallest poppies in his garden before the eyes of his son's messenger, Tarquinius managed to convey to the son that he should put to death or banish the leading men of Gabii. This done, Gabii quickly surrendered to Tarquinius. Kierkegaard quotes the original German.

2. *The Philosophical Works of Descartes*, trans. Elizabeth S. Haldane and G. R. T. Ross, Cambridge University Press, Cambridge, 1973, Vol. I, pp. 231 and 252. Kierkegaard quotes in Latin.

3. ibid., Vol. I, p. 83.

4. 2 Timothy 4.7.

5. A reference to an advertisement in *Berlingske Tidende*, a newspaper run by someone of whom Kierkegaard strongly disapproved and so referred to here slightingly as the 'Advertiser'. In his journals (*Papirer* IV, A 88) he adds, in a comment on the advertisement, that 'the writer should understand that of which he speaks better than the reader, otherwise he shouldn't write'.

6. In J. L. Heiberg's play, *The Reviewer and the Beast*, Trop says, while tearing the manuscript of [his tragedy *The Destruction of the Human Race*] in two equal parts: 'If it doesn't cost more to preserve good taste, why shouldn't we do it?'

7. About three years before the publication of *Fear and Trembling* Copenhagen got its first buses.

8. In saying that Hegel's 'System' would be better described as an omnibus than a tower, Kierkegaard may be alluding to the tower in Luke 14.28–30, referred to in the second of the three *problemata* below, which was not completed because the builder had not 'counted the cost'.

9. Genesis 22.1. See note 53 on 'temptation'. Biblical quotations are from the English Authorized Version, not translations of Kierkegaard's quotations from the Danish.

10. In the journals (*Papirer* III, A 197) Kierkegaard quotes what he

calls a 'quite perfect example of romanticism in the Old Testament, in the Book of Judith 10.11: "And Judith went out, she and her maid with her; but the men of the place watched her until she came down from the mountain, until she came through the valley, and they could see her no more. And they went straight on into the valley".'

11. The expression 'Never a word was spoken of this' occurs in Kierkegaard's journals (e.g. *Papirer* VIII, 1 A 17) in connection with something he learned about, and perhaps from, his father in his early youth. What was never spoken about was whatever Kierkegaard's father took to be the cause of his own morbid melancholy.

12. Kierkegaard's allusions here are to Homer (e.g. *Iliad* vi, 146).

13. Also Homer (e.g. *Iliad* iii, 381, where a god saves a hero by enveloping him in a cloud and carrying him away).

14. 1 Corinthians 3.18. 'If any man among you seemeth to be wise in this world, let him become a fool, that he may be wise.'

15. Hebrews 9.9. 'By faith he sojourned in the land of promise, as in a strange country'.

16. The reference seems to be to Jeremiah, though the Danish editors of the 1963 edition suggest also Ovid, who was exiled on the Black Sea, where he wrote his *Tristia ex Ponto*.

17. Galatians 3.8. 'And the scripture, foreseeing that God would justify the heathen through faith, preached before the gospel unto Abraham, saying, In thee shall all nations be blessed.'

18. Joshua 10.12. 'Then spake Joshua ... and he said in the sight of Israel, Sun, stand thou still upon Gibeon; and thou, Moon, in the valley of Ajalon.'

19. Numbers 20.11–12. 'And Moses ... smote the rock twice: and the water came out abundantly, but the Lord said, Because ye believed me not to sanctify me in the eyes of the children of Israel, therefore ye shall not bring this congregation into the land which I have given them.'

20. Genesis 18.12–13. 'Therefore Sarah laughed within herself, saying, After I am waxed old shall I have pleasure, my lord being old also? And the Lord said unto Abraham, Wherefore did Sarah laugh, saying, Shall I of a surety bear a child, which am old?' But note ibid., 17.17, which says, 'Then Abraham fell upon his face, and laughed, and said in his heart, Shall a child be born unto him that is an hundred years old? and shall Sarah, that is ninety years old, bear?'

21. 'Seventy' seems an arbitrary number. According to Genesis 21.5,

Abraham was a hundred years old when Isaac was born and seventy-five when God first gave him the promise (ibid., 12.4).

22. Genesis 12.2–3. 'And I will make of thee a great nation, and I will bless thee, and make thy name great ... and in thee shall all families of the earth be blessed.'

23. Genesis 18.22 ff. 'And the men turned their faces from thence, and went toward Sodom; but Abraham stood yet before the Lord. And Abraham drew near and said, Wilt thou destroy the righteous with the wicked?'

24. Freely rendered by Kierkegaard after Genesis 22.1.

25. Luke 23.30. 'Then shall they begin to say to the mountains, Fall on us; and to the hills, Cover us.'

26. Genesis 22.3.

27. Freely rendered by Kierkegaard after Genesis 22.3 and 9 f.

28. Genesis 8.4.

29. cf. Plato's *Phaedrus*, 22 and 37.

30. 2 Thessalonians 3.10 and 12. 'For even when we were with you, this we commanded you, that if any would not work, neither should he eat ... Now them that are such we command and exhort, by our Lord Jesus Christ, that with quietness they work, and eat their own bread.'

31. In Oehlenschläger's play *Aladdin*, first produced in Copenhagen in 1839, the hero and Noureddin represent light and darkness respectively. cf. *Papirer* II, A 451.

32. This is Plato's version of the Orpheus legend. See *Symposium* 179d.

33. Matthew 3.9. 'And think not to say within yourselves, We have Abraham to our father: for I say unto you, that God is able of these stones to raise up children unto Abraham.'

34. Isaiah 26.18. 'We have been with child, we have been in pain, we have as it were brought forth wind; we have not wrought any deliverance in the earth ...'

35. Themistocles, as related by Plutarch, *Themistocles*, 3, 3.

36. Matthew 11.28. 'Come unto me, all ye that labour and are heavy laden, and I will give you rest.'

37. Matthew 19.16 ff.

38. It is generally assumed that the reference is indirectly to Regine.

39. From Horace's *Letters*, I, 18, 84: 'It's your affair when the neighbour's house is on fire.'

40. Kierkegaard refers frequently to what he regarded as his physical deformity.

41. Matthew 18.21–2: 'Then came Peter to him, and said, Lord, how oft shall my brother sin against me, and I forgive him? till seven times? Jesus saith unto him, I say not unto thee, Until seven times: but, Until seventy times seven.'

42. John 2.1–10.

43. See note 7.

44. Ephesians 5.16. The passage in the Danish Bible would be rendered in English by 'buying the seasonable time'.

45. It is assumed that Kierkegaard wrote this after hearing of Regine's engagement, an event that had caused him to rewrite the conclusion of *Repetition* in a way that would signal to her his approval. The fact that this passage puts Kierkegaard's response to the engagement in a rather different light would indicate that *Fear and Trembling* was written after *Repetition*, in spite of the order in which they appear in the *Samlede Værker*.

46. From a Danish folk-song.

47. See *Magyarische Sagen, Mährchen und Erzählungen*, by Johann Grafen Mailáth, Stuttgart and Tübingen, 1837, 2nd ed., p. 18. The tale is called 'Erzsi die Spinnerin'. See *Papirer* II, A 449.

48. Horace's *Odes* III, 24, 6: 'cruel necessity of fate'.

49. Matthew 17.20. '... If ye have faith as a grain of mustard seed, ye shall say unto this mountain, Remove hence to yonder place, and it shall remove; and nothing shall be impossible unto you.'

50. Kierkegaard writes in his journals (*Papirer* IV, A 107): 'If I had had faith I would have stayed with Regine.' The entry is dated 17 May 1843.

51. Karl Daub was a contemporary theological writer whose work Kierkegaard comments on in his journals and elsewhere. See *Papirer* IV, A 92.

52. The notion of incommensurability is basically that of the absence of a unit of measure (e.g. length) in terms of which two entities can both be measured exactly. This does not imply incomparability. But in a stronger sense, which Kierkegaard seems to adopt, when two entities are incommensurable (e.g. the individual with reality) they are not strictly comparable at all. In some contexts Kierkegaard treats 'incommensurable' as interchangeable with 'unmeasurable'.

53. 'Temptation' expresses three distinct notions in *Fear and Trembling*, all of them distinguished in the Danish. When God 'tempts' Abraham, God is putting Abraham to a test. The test, however, is Abraham's ability to withstand temptation (*Fristelse*) in another, the usual sense, namely the power of something to attract someone away from a course he or she believes to be the right one. In the present context temptation (*Anfægtelse*) is a state in which someone's being tempted in this usual sense is connected with the idea of passing or failing a test of spiritual adequacy. *Fear and Trembling* contrasts two diametrically opposed applications of this latter: one (as here) in which the individual's pursuit of subjective goals as *moral* ones is to be failing the test from the viewpoint of the Hegelian conviction that public morality is the final court of moral appeal, the other where any appeal to public moral opinion involves a weakening of the 'true' but 'absurd' conviction that the individual can have direct subjective access to an absolute court of moral appeal, in terms of which public morality is reduced to a merely relative status. The context makes clear which of these notions the word 'temptation' expresses, though all three can be seen to be involved in Abraham's case. The test is whether he can resist the temptation to waver in his absolute loyalty to God by seeking public understanding for the act God has commanded, or worse, by invoking the 'universal', e.g. in the form of an appeal to his duty as a father, as an argument against the very idea of an absolute loyalty to God. If Abraham had not loved Isaac as he did, all thought of sacrificing him would have been *Anfægtelse* (see p. 61), because the price paid would be being weighed against some personal advantage. As it was, however, the only such advantages conceivable by Abraham would require him to avoid the sacrifice. Thoughts in *those* directions are *Anfægtelser* for Abraham.

54. 'The Ethical Life' is the title of Part III of Hegel's *Philosophy of Right*, and Kierkegaard's term 'det Sædelige' is a direct translation of 'das Sittliche'. 'Good and Conscience' is the title of a sub-section of Part II. See *Hegel's Philosophy of Right*, trans. T. M. Knox, Oxford University Press, London, 1980, and the present translator's Introduction, above.

55. See, e.g., Hegel's *Phenomenology of Spirit*, trans. A. V. Miller, Clarendon Press, Oxford, 1979, VI, B, Ib, pp. 321 ff.

56. In some of Hegel's earlier writings (see *Theologische Jugendschriften*, ed. by H. Nohl, Tübingen, 1906, p. 247), published late and unavailable to Kierkegaard, Abraham is indeed described in this way.

57. Boileau, *L'art poétique* I, 232.

58. 'Mediation' is the Hegelian term for a process of resolving conceptual oppositions into higher conceptual unities. For instance, the belief that public service conflicts with personal freedom can be 'mediated' (according to Hegel and also Judge William in the second volume of *Either/Or*) in the realization that, properly understood, the latter depends on the former. Because it is a conceptual operation it follows that it occurs 'precisely by virtue of the universal'.

59. Euripides, *Iphigenia in Aulis*, v. 448, in C. Wilster's trans. Agamemnon says, 'How lucky to be born in lowly station where one may be allowed to weep.'

60. Menelaus, Calchas, and Ulysses. cf. ibid., v. 107.

61. ibid., v. 687.

62. Judges 11.30–40. 'And Jephthah vowed a vow unto the Lord, and said, If thou shalt without fail deliver the children of Ammon into mine hands, Then it shall be, that whatsoever cometh forth of the doors of my house to meet me, when I return in peace from the children of Ammon, shall surely be the Lord's, and I will offer it up for a burnt offering ... And Jephthah came to Mizpeh unto his house, and, behold, his daughter came out to meet him with timbrels and with dances ...'

63. While first consul in Rome, L. Junius Brutus put two of his sons to death for trying to restore the Tarquins. Brutus got his name by feigning idiocy in order to escape being murdered by Tarquinius.

64. The ethical life is here, again, Hegel's 'das Sittliche'.

65. In an ironic sense Abraham's act does, then, stand in a relation to the universal. It is directed against the 'families' and 'nations' of which he was to be the father.

66. There is some reason to suppose that the category Kierkegaard has in mind here is faith (see A. Hannay, *Kierkegaard*, Routledge & Kegan Paul, London, 1982, p. 89), in the sense defined in *Concluding Unscientific Postscript*, and specifically a relationship 'unknown to paganism' (cf. *Postscript*, trans. D. F. Swenson and W. Lowrie, Princeton University Press, Princeton, N.J., 1941, p. 496). The trouble with this, however, is that faith in that sense presupposes the concept of sin, which Johannes *de silentio* says he has deliberately excluded from his discussion of Abraham, who 'did not become the single individual through sin' (p. 124 below). So it is unclear how faith will contribute to an understanding of specifically Abraham.

67. See the dedication to Shakespeare's *Sonnets*.

68. Mark 3.22. 'And the scribes which came down from Jerusalem said, He hath Beelzebub, and by the prince of the devils casteth he out devils.'

69. A reference to Hegel's view of the function of the State. See the Introduction, above. For Kierkegaard's most sustained attack on 'levelling', see *A Literary Review*, trans. Alastair Hannay, Penguin Books, London, 2001.

70. Kierkegaard uses the Greek 'skandalon', which in this context means 'stumbling block' or 'offence'. But 'scandal' is apt enough.

71. Genesis 18.11. 'Now Abraham and Sarah were old and well stricken in age; and it ceased to be with Sarah after the manner of women.'

72. Luke 1.38.

73. G. E. Lessing, *Auszüge aus den Literatur-Briefen*, 81st letter, in Maltzahn's ed., Vol. VI, pp. 205 ff.

74. See Hegel's *Logic*, trans. W. Wallace, Clarendon Press, Oxford, 1975, §138, pp. 196–200. The child is 'at first a mere inward' and 'determined' by the 'will of his parents, the attainments of his teachers, and the whole world of reason that environs him' (p. 198). The mature man is determined by the inner in the sense that '[as] a man is outwardly ... so is he inwardly' (p. 197).

75. See *Papirer* I, A 237, where Kierkegaard refers to Schleiermacher and the 'Hegelian dogmatists' who treat faith as a kind of 'vital fluid' or 'atmosphere' to be 'inhaled in spiritual understanding'.

76. C. G. Bretschneider's *Lexicon manuale graeco-latinum in libros N.T.* (1829), Vol. II, p. 87.

77. In Hebrew the feeble consonants ('j' and 'v') are said to 'quiesce', or become silent, when their sound is absorbed in that of a preceding vowel. See *Papirer* II, A 406. Here, however, Kierkegaard has got it the wrong way around.

78. Q. Fabius Maximus, known as Cunctator for his caution in war, was appointed dictator of Rome during the war with Hannibal (217 B.C.) and was five times consul (233–209 B.C.).

79. A chief character in a puppet show. Cf. Kasper and Punch.

80. *Stokkemændene i Gulddaasen*, a play by Olufsen. *Stokkemænd* are people appointed to attend legal proceedings as witnesses.

81. Kierkegaard refers to a 'Dyrehaugsselskab', which, assuming 'Dyrehaug' is the modern 'Dyrehavsbakken', means something like

'zoo company', which might indicate either the visitors to the zoo or its inmates.

82. Corresponding passages are Deuteronomy 13.6 f. and 33.9; Matthew 10.37, 19.29. As a 'similar' passage Kierkegaard inserted in his MS. a reference to 1 Corinthians 7.11, which, however, seems not appropriate.

83. Hegel's *Enzyklopädie*, §384.

84. In his *Logic* (op. cit., §63, p. 99) Hegel equates faith with immediate knowledge, but also with 'inspiration, the heart's revelations, the truths implanted in man by nature, and also in particular, healthy reason or common sense'. Of all these he says they 'agree in adopting as their leading principle the immediacy, or self-evident way, in which a fact or body of truths is presented to consciousness'.

85. Elsewhere Kierkegaard places irony on the boundary between the aesthetic and the ethical, as humour on that between the ethical and the religious. Irony for Kierkegaard is the mode of consciousness in which the finite world as such becomes an object of thought, and thus acquires a certain distance; the 'interesting' can perhaps be related to this in the way that single finite things or persons can, for a consciousness of this kind, assume importance as representatives of the whole in some aspect and degree or other.

86. The Danish here says 'med aesthetisk Inderlighed og Concupiscents', i.e. 'with aesthetic inwardness and concupiscence', but since 'inwardness' can be misleading and 'concupiscence' is old-fashioned I have chosen a more simple rendering.

87. An example of double recognition is where Orestes, who in his attempt to take the statue of Artemis as the price of his recovery from madness has been seized and is to be sacrificed to Artemis, is recognized by, and at the same time recognizes, his sister Iphigenia, whom he believed dead since being sacrificed by Agamemnon but by a devious route had become priestess of Artemis. They escape with Orestes's friend Pylades.

88. Oedipus, in Sophocles's *Oedipus the King*.

89. Iphigenia, in Euripides's *Iphigenia in Tauris*. Agamemnon did not in fact succeed in sacrificing Iphigenia. Artemis put a hart in her place and took her to Tauris where she became priestess. It was there that she later saved her brother from sacrifice.

90. Aristotle, *Natural History*, V, 4, 7. cf. *Papirer* IV, A 36.

91. Euripides, *Iphigenia in Aulis*, op. cit., vv. 861 ff.

92. An argument that takes advantage of the particular features of a situation or person.

93. In Greece an olive branch was the symbol of entreaty.

94. G. E. Lessing, *Hamburgische Dramaturgie* 1. Bd., first and second pieces (Maltzahn's ed., VII, p. 10).

95. Aristotle, *Politics*, 8 (5), 3, 3. Augurs really belong to the Roman priesthood.

96. Kierkegaard believed there was a divine veto against his marriage. The example is obviously one he could view with a great deal of 'aesthetic inwardness and concupiscence' (see note 86). His journals contain reflections that parallel the possibilities listed here.

97. Axel and Valborg were forbidden by the Church to marry owing to their close consanguinity.

98. See Lessing, op. cit., 1. Bd., twenty-second piece (Maltzahn's ed., VII, p. 96).

99. The legend occurs in a folk-song and has been used by Jens Baggesen in his *Agnete from Holmegaard*, as well as by Hans Christian Andersen in his dramatic poem *Agnete and the Merman*, first produced (disastrously) at the Royal Danish Theatre in 1843.

100. In fact it doesn't, while the fairy-tale of 'Beauty and the Beast' (Molbech, No. 7) does.

101. Kierkegaard remarks repeatedly (especially *Postscript*, op. cit., pp. 359 ff. etc.) that the monastic movement of the Middle Ages was a mistaken, 'abstract' way of relating oneself to the 'absolute *telos*'.

102. Lacking the necessary condition for the attainment of the highest good is the situation Kierkegaard equates with 'hereditary' sin. In it the primary problem is to establish a relationship to the 'absolute *telos*', which is a matter for the individual as such and not as an instance of the universal.

103. The Book of Tobit is among the apocrypha of the Old Testament.

104. See Schiller's *Resignation*, 3rd strophe.

105. Longus was a Greek sophist in the 4th or 5th century A.D., and author of *Daphnis and Chloë*, an erotic piece that is extant.

106. Book of Tobit, 7.18–20.

107. Shakespeare, *King Richard III*, Act I, Scene 1. Kierkegaard in fact quotes the German translation, since he could not read English.

108. Stepmothers were traditionally attributed evil influences over their stepchildren.

109. The poet Cumberland's play *The Jew* was performed frequently at the Royal Danish Theatre between 1795 and 1834. Scheva

the Jew was thought by everyone to be a miser and usurer, but in secret he was a great benefactor.

110. In Jens Baggesen's *Kirkegaarden in Sobradise* (*Danske Værker*, I, p. 282).

111. Aristotle according to Seneca, *De tranquillitate animi*, Dial. IX, 17, 10. cf. *Papirer* I, A 148.

112. Tamerlane, king of the Mongolians 1370–1405, a conqueror famed for his cruelty.

113. The honour of destruction. Herostratus set fire to the temple of Artemis at Ephesus the same night that Alexander the Great was born (356 B.C.), in order to make himself immortal.

114. Gregorius Rimini, an Augustinian monk who was Professor of Philosophy in the University of Paris and died in 1358, was given this name because he subscribed to the view that unbaptized children went to hell, not limbo as usually held among Catholics.

115. Ludvig Holberg's *Erasmus Montanus*, Act I, Scene 3. A character, the deacon, says, in connection with bargaining for the price of the earth to be cast on a grave, 'I can say to a peasant, "Will you have fine sand or just earth?"'

116. Matthew 6.17–18.

117. Commentators link this notion, the 'idea of the congregation', to the populist religious movement led by Nikolai Frederik Severin Grundtvig (1783–1872). According to Grundtvig, Christianity was based on the 'living word from the Lord's own mouth' in the ceremonies of confession, and not on the Bible, which was open to attack.

118. Kierkegaard's word is 'desultorisk', or 'desultorily' in the sense of 'skippingly' or 'disconnectedly'. Perhaps 'from different points of view'.

119. *King Richard III*, Act II, Scene 1. Again Kierkegaard quotes the German translation.

120. I Corinthians 14.23.

121. Genesis 22.8.

122. Plato's *Apology*, 36 A. Some texts read 'thirty votes'.

123. Diogenes Laertius, of Laërte, in Cilicia, most likely lived in the 2nd century A.D. Author of the *Lives of the Philosophers*, in ten books.

124. 'The Tailor in Heaven', Grimms' *Fairy Tales*, Vol. I, 2nd ed. (1819), p. 177. According to the Grimms, however, the tailor was really dead.

125. The disciple was Cratylus, an Athenian contemporary of Socrates.

CHRONOLOGY

1756   Michael Pedersen Kierkegaard, Søren's father, born in formal bondage of peasant stock in Sæding, West Jutland. Baptized 12 December.

1768   Michael Kierkegaard apprenticed to his uncle, a hosier, in Copenhagen. Ane Sørensdatter Lund, Søren's mother, born 18 June in south-east Jutland.

1777   The Sæding village priest formally releases Michael Kierkegaard from serfdom.

1788   Michael Kierkegaard receives royal patent 'to deal in East Indian and Chinese goods, as well as goods coming from our West Indian islands ... and to sell same at wholesale or retail to all and sundry'. This was the year that Arthur Schopenhauer was born.

1794   Michael Kierkegaard marries Kirstine Røyen, sister of a business partner.

1796   23 March, Kirstine Røyen Kierkegaard dies childless; Michael Kierkegaard inherits from his uncle and benefactor.

1797   Michael Kierkegaard retires from business in February. On 26 April, he marries Kirstine's maid, and his own distant cousin, Ane Sørensdatter Lund, at the family home on Købmagergade in Copenhagen. A daughter, Maren Kirstine, is born 7 September.

1799   25 October, a second daughter, Nicoline Christine, is born.

1801   7 September, a third, Petrea Severine, is born.

1805   A first son, Peter Christian, is born.

1807   23 March, a second son, Søren Michael, is born.

1808   The year in which Hans Lassen Martensen, Kierkegaard's tutor to be, rival and bitter opponent, was born.

1809   30 April, a third son, Niels Andrea, is born.

1813   5 May, a last child, Søren Aabye, is born at home (2 Nytorv), and baptized in the Church of the Holy Spirit

3 June. This was the year the State Bank was declared bank-
rupt, as a result of economic problems stemming from the
bombardment of Copenhagen by the British fleet in 1807
and Denmark's continuing alliance with Napoleon. Other
notable figures born that year were the composers Richard
Wagner and Giuseppe Verdi.

1819   14 September, Kierkegaard's brother Søren Michael dies,
       aged twelve.

1821   Kierkegaard begins school at Copenhagen's Borger-
       dydskole.

1822   15 March, Maren Kirstine, Michael Kierkegaard's favourite
       daughter, dies, aged twenty-four.

1823   15 February, Regine Olsen, Kierkegaard's future fiancée, is
       born.

1828   20 April, Kierkegaard is confirmed in the Church of Our
       Lady by Pastor (later Bishop) J. P. Mynster.

1830   The year of the July Revolution, a three-day revolt in Paris
       that ends the Bourbon restoration, with its tightened con-
       trol of the press and universities, and results in some degree
       of liberal reform. In Denmark, as elsewhere, one effect of the
       revolt was to consolidate the lobby for freedom of the press.
       Kierkegaard, who later takes part in the dispute over press
       freedom, graduates from the Borgerdydskole (with distinc-
       tion in Greek, history, French and Danish composition) and
       on 30 October enters the University of Copenhagen. On 1
       November he enlists in the King's Lifeguard, but four days
       later is discharged as unfit for service. His brother Peter
       Christian (known in academic circles as 'the disputing devil
       of the North'), who was in Paris at the time of the July
       Revolution, receives a doctorate from the University of
       Göttingen for a dissertation on telling lies.

1831   25 April, Kierkegaard takes the first part of the first-year
       university exam (with distinction in Latin, Greek, Hebrew,
       and history, and exceptional distinction in lower mathe-
       matics), and on 27 October the second part (with excep-
       tional distinction in all subjects: theoretical and practical
       philosophy, physics and higher mathematics). This was the
       year that Hegel, whose influence on Danish philosophy

provoked Kierkegaard's later onslaught on Hegelianism, died.

1832 Kierkegaard's 33-year-old sister Nicoline Christine (married to a clothier, Johan Christian Lund) dies after childbirth.

1832 His brother Niels Andreas emigrates to the USA to pursue a business career.

1833 21 September, Niels Andreas dies, twenty-four years old, in Paterson, New Jersey.

1834 31 July, his mother dies. 4 December, he makes his journalistic debut, under the imprint 'A', with a piece in *Flyveposten* (The Flying Post) entitled 'Also a Defence of Woman's Superior Capacity', in response to an article on the same theme. 29 December, his sister Petrea Severine (married to a banker, Heinrich Ferdinand Lund) dies after childbirth. Friedrich Schleiermacher, the Christian theologian and philosopher, also died this year, having visited and been fêted in Copenhagen only the year before.

1835 He spends a summer holiday at Gilleleje in northern Sjælland. Records his resolve 'to find a truth that is true for me, to find the idea for which I am willing to live and die.' 28 November, he reads a paper to the Student Union on 'Our Journal Literature' with reference to freedom of the press.

1836 He publishes (in *Flyveposten* and under the imprint 'B', but finally under his own name) three articles in an exchange on the topic of the paper delivered to the Student Union. Later in the year, his surviving brother Peter Christian marries and the couple make their home at 2 Nytorv.

1837 In May, he meets Regine Olsen (then fifteen years old) for the first time while visiting the Rørdam family in Frederiksberg. In September, he begins teaching Latin at the Borgerdysdskole and moves from Nytorv to his own apartment at 7 Løvstraede. In July, Peter Christian's young wife dies.

1838 13 March, Kierkegaard's mentor and mainstay, Poul Martin Møller, dies at forty-four. 9 August, his father dies and he inherits a sum amounting to near half a million dollars. In September he publishes his first book, *From the*

Papers of One Still Living, attacking Hans Christian Andersen.

1839–40 He studies assiduously. In the winter he moves into an apartment at 11 Kultorvet, which he shares with another student. Ten months later he moves again, to 230A (now 38) Nørregade.

1840 He finally passes his examination for the theological degree (with distinction, though not at the top of the class), visits his ancestral home in Jutland, and, 10 September (having 'approached her for a month'), proposes to Regine Olsen, who is now eighteen years old to his twenty-seven. She accepts. In November, Kierkegaard enters the pastoral seminary for practical training in the ministry.

1841 12 January, he preaches a sermon in Holmen's Church. In July, his dissertation for the M.A. (later Ph.D.) degree. 'On the Concept of Irony', is accepted for public defence. 11 August, he breaks his engagement to Regine. 29 September, he successfully defends his dissertation. 11 October, the break with Regine is complete; 25 October, he leaves by ship for Berlin. He attends Schelling's lectures in Berlin, among others.

1842 Having written large parts of *Either/Or* in Berlin, he returns in March to Copenhagen to complete the work. Begins, but does not complete, or publish, 'De Omnibus Dubitandum Est'. Copenhagen this year saw the birth of Georg Brandes, a Danish intellectual who was to become an internationally famous literary critic and tried too late to interest Nietzsche in Kierkegaard's work.

1843 15 February, *Either/Or* published. May, he briefly visits Berlin. 8 May, two days before his departure, *Two Edifying Discourses* was published, followed 7 October by *Fear and Trembling* and *Repetition*, 13 October by *Three Edifying Discourses*, and 6 December by *Four Edifying Discourses*.

1844 24 February, Kierkegaard held, in the Church of the Trinity, and with 'distinction', the trial sermon required for entry into the Danish Church. *Two Edifying Discourses* and *Three Edifying Discourses* were published 5 March and 8 June respectively. Then in June *Philosophical Fragments*, *The*

Concept of Anxiety, and *Prefaces*. In August followed *Four Edifying Discourses*. In October, he moves from 230A Nørregade back to the family house at 2 Nytorv. In the wider world, on which these works would later have some impact, this year saw the birth of Friedrich Nietzsche, whose father was born the same year as Kierkegaard.

1845 *Three Discourses on Imagined Occasions* and *Stages on Life's Way* are published in April on successive days. In May, he is away for two weeks on a brief visit to Berlin.

1846 In January, *The Corsair*, responding to a provocation signed by one of Kierkegaard's pseudonyms, attacks him in person. He briefly considers becoming a country pastor. *Concluding Unscientific Postscript* is published 27 February, followed on 30 March by *A Literary Review*. In May, he is absent once more from Copenhagen for a two-week trip to Berlin. In October, Meyer Goldschmidt, the editor of *The Corsair* and formerly a protégé of Kierkegaard, resigns and leaves Denmark.

1847 13 March, *Edifying Discourses in a Different Tenor* is published; 29 September, *Works of Love*. His publisher informs him that *Either/Or* is sold out. On 16 May, his rival and former tutor, Hans Lassen Martensen, is appointed Royal Chaplain. On 3 November, Regine marries her former teacher Friedrich Schlegel. In December, Kierkegaard sells the family home a 2 Nytorv. During the year he has twice visited his brother, now remarried and pastor at an out-of-town-parish at Pedersborg, near Sorø. Abroad, Marx and Engels are drafting the *Communist Manifesto*, which came out the following year.

1848 The year of the February Revolution in France with repercussions throughout Europe. These include the Dano-Prussian war over Schleswig-Holstein. His servant is drafted. Just previously, 20 January, King Christian VIII, with whom Kierkegaard had at least two audiences, had died. On 28 January, he had signed a lease on an apartment at the corner of Rosenborggade and Tornebuskgade and in April moved in. On 26 April, *Christian Discourses* is published and 24 and 27 July the two-part article, 'The Crisis

and a Crisis in an Actress's Life'. By November he has finished *The Point of View of My Work as an Author* but decides
not to have it published in his lifetime. The year was also
the gestation period for *The Sickness unto Death*, some conception for which is first mentioned in a journal entry from
28 December 1847.

1849   *The Lilies of the Field and the Birds of the Air* and *Two Minor
Ethico-Religious Treatises* are published 14 and 19 May
respectively. *The Sickness unto Death* is published 30 July
under a new pseudonym, Anti-Climacus, and *Three
Discourses at Communion on Fridays* 13 November.

1850   18 April, he moves to yet another apartment, at 43
Nørregade. *Practice in Christianity* is published under the
Anti-Climacus pseudonym 27 September and *An Edifying
Discourse* 20 December.

1851   In April, he moves outside the old city's walls to 108A
Østerbro. On 18 May he gave a sermon at the Citadel
Church, in August published *Two Discourses at Communion
on Fridays* and *On My Work as an Author*, and 10 September
For Self-Examination.

1852–3   In April, he moves back inside the city to a small two-
room flat let out of a larger apartment at Klaedeboderne 5–6
(now 28 Skindergade and 5 Dyrkøb), just opposite the
Church of Our Lady. *Judge for Yourself* is completed but not
published until twenty-one years after his death. In his
journals he reflects over his 'life's operation'.

1854   30 January, Bishop Mynster dies. In February, Kierkegaard
writes an article attacking the established church, but does
not publish it until December. Hans Martensen is named
Bishop 15 April. Rather than provoking reaction, publication of the article causes some confusion.

1855   From January to the end of May, he attacks the church in
various articles published in *Faedrelandet*. In this final year
he publishes: 24 May, *This Must Be Said, So Let It Now Be
Said*; 16 June, *Christ's Judgment on Official Christianity*; and 3
September, *The Unchangeableness of God*. In May he begins
his own broadsheet, *The Instant*. It goes through nine issues
before he falls ill. On 2 October, he collapses outside his

home and is taken later, at his own request, to Frederiks Hospital. He dies there six weeks later, at 9 p.m., 11 November, probably of a staphylococcus infection of the lungs, though there was no autopsy. His funeral, at the prompting of his brother Peter Christian, but much to Martensen's distaste, was conducted at the Church of Our Lady, attracting people of all classes, while the burial itself was the occasion of a disturbance in which Kierkegaard's devoted but overwrought nephew deplored the fact that the Church (at his older uncle's instigation) had commandeered the proceedings.

1859 *The Point of View of my Authorship* is published by Peter Christian Kierkegaard.

1860 The death of Arthur Schopenhauer (b. 1788), whose works Kierkegaard first read with admiration and mixed appreciation in 1854.

1884 Hans Lassen Martensen dies.

1888 24 February, Peter Christian Kierkegaard dies, aged eighty-two, his mind unbalanced. Thirteen years earlier, he resigned his episcopate in Aalborg (1856–75) and resigned his civic rights, placing himself in legal custody.

1904 Regine Schlegel dies. Her husband, Fritz Schlegel, governor of the Danish West Indies from 1855 until 1860 (on his deathbed Kierkegaard jibed that Regine had always wanted to be a 'governess') and later an important city official in Copenhagen, had died in 1896.